**PARACELSUS
VAN HELMONT
ANTON MESMER
BARON CARL VON REICHENBACH
MARY BAKER EDDY
DR. WILHELM REICH
PROFESSOR J. B. RHINE**

What do these names—and many others on the roll call of the centuries—share in common?

All were brilliant figures.

All were branded as impostors, frauds, or even worse.

And all believed in a mysterious force permeating the universe, whether it was called "animal magnetism," "odyle," "orgone energy," "radiation," "ESP" or simply "the X force."

In the amazing yet absolutely authentic cases that follow, this force will come to vivid, undeniable life before the reader's eyes. Be warned and prepare yourself . . .

"Fascinating exploration . . . written with grace and verve"
    —THE (LANSING, MICH.) STATE JOURNAL

POWERS THAT BE

By BEVERLEY NICHOLS

POPULAR LIBRARY • NEW YORK

All POPULAR LIBRARY books are carefully selected by the POPULAR LIBRARY Editorial Board and represent titles by the world's greatest authors.

POPULAR LIBRARY EDITION

Copyright © Beverley Nichols 1966
Library of Congress Catalog Card Number: 65-23600

Published by arrangement with St. Martin's Press, Inc.
St. Martin's Press edition published in May, 1966

PRINTED IN THE UNITED STATES OF AMERICA
All Rights Reserved

1. A FIRE IN HIS HANDS

On the second occasion I thought it wise to take along a witness. There was a chance that we might be assisting at a miracle; I wanted some independent testimony.

She was a shrewd old neighbour of mine—we will call her Lady D.—who has often startled me by the clarity of her analysis of characters and situations. The very old and the very young have the same clairvoyance; you can trust their first impressions.

She sat next to me on the sofa. Dr Ash sat on a stool in front of us. I rolled up my sleeve and laid my arm on the table.

'Before we begin,' I said, 'are you sure it's all right for my friend to sit so close? Whatever is going to happen may be pretty powerful.'

Dr Ash smiled. He was remembering what I had just told him about Lady D.'s experience on the night before. I had been round to talk to her about him, and I had read her the last few pages of his book.* When I had finished she had complained—no, that is not the right word—she had *reported* a sensation of acute tingling in both her hands. After I had left her, this tingling had spread all over her body, to such an extent that she had become alarmed and had sent for her own doctor. She was afraid that there might be something wrong with her heart. But her heart was as sound as a bell; there was no sort of physiological disturbance, merely this inexplicable—but not disagreeable—tingling, from tip to toe.

* Dr Michael Ash, M.R.C.S., L.R.C.P., *Health, Radiation & Healing* (Mackay & Co. Ltd, 1962).

5

All this, of course, may sound faintly ridiculous. Many things in this book will sound ridiculous—almost as ridiculous as the things one reads in the newspapers.

'There is nothing to be afraid of,' said Dr Ash.

'I am not in the least afraid,' observed Lady D. rather tartly.

I was still not quite ready. 'I think I should explain that I'm not going out of my way to help. I'm not going to struggle against it, but I'm not going to push it along.' I looked at my outstretched hand. 'I'm trying to imagine that this wretched thing doesn't belong to me. If it does anything, it will be doing it because it can't help doing it, not because I told it to.'

'Supposing we relax,' said the doctor. He moved a little closer and stretched out his arm. His hands were now about six inches from my own.

'Anyway,' I said finally, 'nothing may happen at all.'

But fifteen seconds later it was happening. First the familiar swelling in the veins from the shoulder to the wrist. Then the twitching and the shivering of the skin all over the hand. Then the feeling of a network of delicate bones and tissues straining to get into position. I was suddenly reminded of a rather gruesome film I had once seen of a dead frog that had been re-animated by a charge of electricity.

I must go back again for a moment. Two years before, I had been nearly killed in a motor accident. Among the various injuries were a couple of broken fingers and a splintered wrist. These were never set by the hospital to which I was taken. When I expressed to the orthopedic surgeon my fear that I might never again be able to play the piano I was told to go straight home and play it and not to make a fuss. After a month of agony I went to one of those people who are described by one's friends as 'the top man in Harley Street'. He pursed his lips, shook his head, and informed me that it was too late for him to do anything, and that there was nothing for it but physiotherapy. I had physiotherapy—and more physiotherapy; and hot wax baths and massage and radiant heat; and though they seemed to do me no harm, neither did they do me much good. The agony lessened and gradually I could use a pen to write with, but I was seldom altogether free from pain. And the scherzos of Chopin were gathering dust on the top of the piano.

So here I was, with my arm bare to the elbow, and a man stretching out his arms—not touching me, making no physical contact whatsoever—and my hand performing these ex-traordinary antics.

Dr Ash spoke softly. 'It's very strong today.'

I nodded. 'Yes. There's a word for what my hand's doing but I can't think of it. I shall, in a moment.'

I stared straight ahead of me. I was concentrating on *not* helping; it was very vital that there should be no question of self-hypnosis. Even more important to banish from one's mind any suggestion of faith-healing. I did not want to have faith. All I wanted was to be assured beyond any shadow of doubt, while I was in a state of complete awareness and clarity of mind, that an unseen force was *compelling* part of my body to react in a manner so physically unmistakable that those reactions could be analysed, measured and, if neces-sary, photographed.

The next glance at my hand gave me that assurance. Things were happening which I could not possibly have achieved of my own volition. Lady D. saw them too. I heard her whisper . . . 'It's a miracle.' Well, it was. For the skin was vibrating like a cord of elastic after you have stretched it and let it go. And the fingers too. If you are a pianist, and if your trills are up to standard, you can do some pretty fast work with your fingers. But now my fingers were doing a sort of supersonic trill . . . and they were doing it, remember, *of their own accord*, with no instructions from my own brain, to an unwritten music, drifting down into this quiet room— from where?

This had been going on for precisely four minutes. I had checked my watch because I wanted to remind myself that I was doing a job of reporting. Incidentally, there is a report-er's item in the position of the watch itself. It was on the sofa beside me. Dr Ash had asked me to take it off my wrist because the force that came from his hands was so powerful that it made watches go haywire.

What else should I be noting? With the mise en scène I was already familiar. We were sitting in the parlour of a large Edwardian house in the North London suburb of Enfield. The room was dimly lit and the walls were crowded with religious pictures, mostly of New Testament subjects. There was a pretty garden outside. The house itself belonged to two kindly ladies who had offered it to Dr Ash as the head-quarters of a healing centre.

What else for the reporter's notebook? Perhaps I should spotlight the leading man, as he sits on the stool before me, holding out his hands. Dr Ash is in his early forties. He is tall and dark and 'good-looking' in the most literal sense; he is not only handsome, he gives out a 'vibration' of virtue. The very last thing he suggests is any sort of crankiness or hocus-pocus. Well . . . why should he? After all, his medical record is impeccable, even though he has frequently caused a number of eyebrows to be very sharply raised in the British Medical Association. His personal background is equally unassailable; he is a devout Catholic, happily married with a large family, and the least mercenary individual I have ever met. The main criticism orthodoxy makes against him is that he is too inclined to hit the headlines, as on the occasion when, in the summer of 1962, he claimed to have a sweet-meat endowed with the power to counteract the effects of atomic fall-out. Periodicals like *Life* magazine in America were condescendingly contemptuous of his contentions, largely, I suspect, because nobody had taken the trouble—as a few of us did—to study the deeply impressive evidence behind them. However, Ash goes on his way undisturbed, whether he hits the headlines or not. For he does not care about headlines; he only cares, most passionately, for the Truth.

What else? Here I must revert to my own physical condition at this moment. I was beginning to sweat very hard. I would not mention this not very pretty detail if it did not seem to have significance. Why this phenomenon? The room was cool, I had taken my jacket off, I was sitting quite still and, anyway, I am not a great sweater because I have no superfluous flesh.

And yet, I might have been in a Turkish bath. Why? Mental excitement? True, I was mentally excited, but that is not how mental excitement affects me. I do not have to get out a handkerchief and wipe my forehead when Rubinstein is playing the Rachmaninoff B minor.

One last detail. (The watch showed that we had now been at it for six minutes.) I was becoming physically exhausted. Moreover, the whole arm from the shoulder to the finger-tips was aching almost unbearably. I was moving no muscles and was totally relaxed, but I was suffering the same sharp pains that result from an over-indulgence in violent physical exercise.

I said to Ash: 'Do you mind if we stop now?'

He let his arms drop to his side. As he did so my own hand gave a last flutter and came to rest. It was as though somebody had switched off the electricity.

I got out the handkerchief and wiped my face. 'I think I've found the word I wanted—for what my hand was doing.'

'Yes?'

'It was protesting.'

Dr Ash said nothing.

'Well, that was what it felt like. All those bones and muscles writhing up and down. They didn't seem to *want* to do what they were doing.'

'I wouldn't say that. They were trying to get back to normal. And in your condition that means quite a struggle.'

But it was Lady D. who found the right words for it. 'To me', she said, 'it was like the casting out of devils.'

2. NEW WORDS FOR OLD WORLDS

All things, by immortal power,
Near or far,
Hiddenly
To each other linked are,
That thou canst not stir a flower
Without troubling of a star.

FRANCIS THOMPSON

'A thing that is worth doing at all', wrote G. K. Chesterton, 'is worth doing badly.' Which is perhaps only another way of saying *le mieux est l'ennemi du bien.*

I shall probably write this book badly. The matters with which it will attempt to deal are of great mystery and infinite range, and even the vocabulary which I shall be obliged to use presents unaccustomed problems, because the English language has not yet caught up with some of the activities of the men and women whom we shall be meeting.

Consider the word 'radiesthesia', to which we shall have frequent recurrence. Although radiesthesia in its various forms has been practised for many years, and has given rise to a considerable body of literature in many languages, it has not yet attained the distinction of being included in the Oxford Dictionary. However, we can at least find the basis for a definition in a recent book by Brian Inglis, called *Fringe Medicine,* which carries a foreword by G. M. Carstairs, Professor of Psychological Medicine at the University of Edinburgh.* In a long chapter devoted entirely to radiesthesia he describes it as 'basically nothing more than an attempt to apply to medicine the techniques used in water-divining or dowsing'. Although this is a considerable over-simplification we shall do well to bear it in mind as a sort of lowest common denominator of many other definitions. Thus, the members of the British Medical Society for the Study of Radiesthesia usually content themselves by observing that 'it is the name given to human sensitivity to and perception of radiation' . . . though when they develop this theme they branch off

* Brian Inglis, *Fringe Medicine* (Faber & Faber, London, 1964).

into a great many obscure variations. Many of these variations are probably due to the fact that the majority of practising radiesthetists in modern Britain are not qualified doctors, and are obliged to make up their own terms of reference as they go along. Apart from this, as Brian Inglis observes, radiesthesia is 'an art rather than a craft, and consequently not easily analysed or tested'. (A limitation which, after all, applies with equal cogency to the art of the musician!)

From these scattered fragments let us compose our own definition even though it may not be final nor authoritative:

> *Radiesthesia.* A term derived from the French *Radiesthésie* to describe a technique of therapy based on the largely accepted principles of water-divining in its application to the human, animal and vegetable kingdoms. In general, human sensitivity to those 'radiations' which, according to certain schools of thought from Mesmer downwards, emanate from all living things.

So much for our definition, which obviously covers a multitude of mysteries. Nobody, to my knowledge, has yet gathered all these mysteries under the same cover, nor tried, however painfully and inadequately, to define their common denominator. Nobody has endeavoured to explain the link between the power that flashed from Mesmer's fingers with the power that sparkles from buried waters into the fingers of the dowser—the same power that flows into flowers from the fingers of those who are born with 'green thumbs'—the same power that surges *corporately* from a great orchestra into the physical person of a great artist. To illustrate the almost frighteningly wide range of the radiesthetic theme, I would like to mention a brief conversation with Sir Malcolm Sargent after a concert that he had conducted at the Royal Albert Hall. He had asked me to witness a rehearsal of William Walton's *Belshazzar's Feast*, a work that makes almost brutal demands on the physical stamina of the conductor. At the end of it he came back to his dressing-room and threw himself into a chair. He reminded me of an athlete exhausted after a grilling race. Curiously I asked him: 'What would happen if your body had to go through all these motions in solitude and in silence?' Without hesitation, and certainly without irony he replied, 'I should drop dead.' I believe that to be literally true and I believe the sustaining power that comes from the music and from the corporate emotions of the players to be the same as the sustaining power that flows from the fingers of Michael Ash.

We speak loosely of 'crowd psychology' and freely admit that persons caught up in the passions of crowds are constantly seen to perform actions, good or bad, of which they would be physically and mentally incapable as individuals. Why? I believe that there is a 'radiesthetic' explanation of this mystery—for mystery it is. I have even heard it suggested, by one particularly enthusiastic radiesthetist, that a 'corporate' *silence,* such as the two-minute silence with which we used to commemorate Armistice Day, was actually more 'silent' than the mere absence of sounds.

Will this be difficult to prove? I suspect that it will be very difficult indeed. One of the problems that faces the pioneer research-worker in the field of radiesthesia is the fact that many of the men who ought to be working together are in fact working against one another. Consider the case of spiritual healers. There is overwhelming evidence, which I have quoted in a later chapter, that a man like Harry Edwards is a born healer and an exceptionally sensitive conductor of the power which we have been discussing. But he insists on denying this power and attributes it all to the departed spirits of Pasteur and Lister. He claims that these eminent gentlemen are personally guiding his fingers from the lofty eminence of a sort of Elysian Harley Street. He denies a great miracle, of which there is abundant proof, and postulates a minor miracle, of which there is no proof whatsoever. That he sincerely believes in this minor miracle I have no doubt, but I deplore his belief. Of its very nature it contracts an Infinite Circle to the stuffy confines of a private séance.

Consider again the case of Christian Science . . . a prickly subject, if ever there was one. If any body of men or women ought at least to examine the claims of radiesthesia it is the Christian Scientists. For though true radiesthesia —or sensitivity to physical radiations—is purely physical in origin and reflex, its territory seems constantly to overlap into psychic regions, such as map-dowsing, in which the power of mind over matter is clearly demonstrated. And if the Christian Scientists do not believe in the power of mind over matter—or what we erroneously regard as matter— what do they believe in? The whole point of the story I told in Chapter One was that an unseen power had a very definite effect on *matter*—that it caused muscles to move, skin to vibrate and bones to twitch—and that it did this without any psychological intervention or 'conditioning'. But the Christian Scientists tell us that all these movings and vibratings and twitchings must have been illusions and as much an error as the pain they were struggling to eliminate. Which is really too silly to argue about. If you follow that argument to its logical conclusion you end up by denying the miracles of Christ.

Which reminds me. At the end of Michael Ash's book—much of which is too technical for most of us to understand—the contemplation of this power gives wings to his pen, and he writes a passage which is not only beautiful in itself but contains—whether you are a Christian or a Buddhist or a Muslim or a nothing at all—the whole theory and practice of radiesthesia:

> Famous agnostics, such as Shaw, have spoken of a belief in the 'life force' without being able to determine its real source and purpose. The power of radiation which I have been considering, has a universality and a potency which agnostics might think equates it to their 'life force', and the little we already know about its manifestation would support such a comparison. But because of my conviction about the source from which this power stems, my personal belief goes a great deal farther. For I believe this is the power which has created everything that is out of an empty void and without whose support everything would again vanish into nothingness.

> This is the power that drives the world on its course through space and is the most potent force on earth.

> In this power we are faced with the formative force which pervades all forms of matter and accounts for its inexpressible beauty, which alters material things and makes them always new, which drives life up from the soil and which fashions us from the womb.

> I believe this power operates only for the good of us all, cannot be deflected to our own ends, and can guide us in every act we make. Without it we are hollow shells; with it we fulfil the purpose for which we are made, and can be channels through which we heal the sick.

> This is the power which works through prayer and which shines in the haloes of saints.

This is the power which so filled Jesus that the very hem of his garment was alive with it.

What are my own qualifications for attempting a survey of these mysteries?

Firstly, I think, the fact that I am among the small minority who has actually witnessed the performance of a miracle on his own body.

This fact, I hope, may in some degree compensate for my lack of scientific training. Supposing that a miracle were performed on the body of a very ordinary man in the presence of a number of distinguished scientists, and supposing that a reporter were sent to write an account of it, the story from the lips of the man himself would be of considerably greater interest—however haltingly it might be told—than all the theories of all the scientists of the world. To put it crudely, the syndication of 'Lazarus' Own Story', from the lips of Lazarus himself, would attract a wider public than anything that Schweitzer might have to say about it.

My second qualification for writing this book, however inadequately, is that for a number of years I have been perhaps more interested than the average layman in the phenomena which it discusses. The first published intimation of this interest was proclaimed in a play called *Mesmer*, which the late Sir Charles Cochran produced with a distinguished cast in the year 1938. It was not a very good play, and it soon 'folded'. However, with all its faults, there were dramatic situations in it—radiesthetic situations of such innate force that I have often wished that some other dramatist would take up where I left off, telling the story as it should be told to the audience that it deserves.

Mesmer, and the modern inheritors of the school of therapy with which his name is commonly associated, we shall be meeting in due course. Meanwhile, I should like to tell a story.

Mesmer had more than a little of the Barnum about him. If he had been a contemporary of our own instead of a contemporary of Mozart—who honoured him with his friendship and improvised in his candle-lit garden—we might well have seen his name in bright lights above the entrance to a music hall. This flair for showmanship has clouded his historical image; we cannot see the man for the props; we cannot hear his message clearly because of the theatrical manner of its delivery. This difficulty to assess him at his proper value must have been even more acute in his own day and age . . . but I was supposed to be telling a story.

The historical climax of Mesmer's career centred round a little pianist with the pretty name of Thérèse Paradis. As an infant prodigy she had attracted the attention of Mozart, who had caused her to perform before the Empress Maria Theresa. By the time she was in her late teens she was a considerable celebrity. And then, of a sudden, she was struck blind. We have no precise medical details of the cause of this blindness, but there is a good deal of indirect evidence to suggest that it was the result of an overwhelming nervous shock at a moment when her eyes, which were never very strong, were close to a bright light. This at least was Mesmer's opinion when—after her case had been given up as hopeless by the entire medical fraternity—she was at last brought to him by Mozart. He announced that he could cure her. Here was a situation tense with drama; on the one side a figure of appealing pathos championed by an erratic genius, on the other the outraged forces of orthodox medicine proclaiming that the genius was a dangerous crank. The drama mounted as the light began to flicker back into Thérèse's eyes under Mesmer's treatment, which was pure and simple radiesthesia. All this is a matter of history. It is also a matter of history that Mesmer was eventually summoned to defend himself before the most powerful board of doctors that could be assembled from the whole of Europe, one of whom, by the way, bore the sinister name of Dr Guillotin. It is only during this final speech in his own defence that I allowed myself a certain amount of dramatic licence, and even then the main burden of his pleading is an almost literal transcription of passages from his own works.

Dr Lamettrie, one of the court physicians, in a series of repeated assaults, had been trying to force Mesmer to define in conventional medical terminology the force that flowed from his fingers. Even today such a definition would be difficult; in the eighteenth century, when such matters were relegated to the realms of witchcraft and black magic, it was well-nigh impossible.

The dialogue went like this:

DR LAMETTRIE (*acidly*). Now, Doctor Mesmer—about this 'magnetism' of yours. Tell us—can it be seen?

MESMER. No.

DR LAMETTRIE. Has it a smell?

MESMER. No.

DR LAMETTRIE. Is it to be weighed?

MESMER. No.

DR LAMETTRIE. Touched?

MESMER. No.

DR LAMETTRIE. Measured?

MESMER. No.

DR LAMETTRIE. Tasted?

MESMER. No.

DR LAMETTRIE. Observed under the microscope?

MESMER. No.

DR LAMETTRIE (*looking round*). Well—gentlemen—I *ask* you!

MESMER (*quickly*). And I will ask *you* something, doctor. Have you a soul?

DR LAMETTRIE. A soul? I hope so.

MESMER. And if so, has it a smell?

(*General laughter.*)

MESMER. And is your soul to be weighed, touched, measured, tasted, observed under the microscope? Gentlemen— I ask *you*.

DR GUILLOTIN (*absently*). Just because we can't see Dr Lamettrie's soul under the microscope, we mustn't deny that he has one. It might be a very *small* soul.

DR LEROI. Dr Guillotin—for the last time!

DR LAMETTRIE (*loudly and emphatically*). I insist upon concrete proof of the existence of magnetism.

MESMER (*desperately*). But how can I give you concrete proof of something that is intangible? Do not ask the impossible of me, gentlemen. Do not ask me to bottle the spirit of the Universe, and to show it to you! Would you have me draw sparks from my fingers? Would that convince you? Would you have me draw down lightning—in order to prove that it is *there*? You *know* it is there, in the heavens, like a sword that is sheathed, waiting for God to draw it.

DR D'ESLON. We only wish to find out the facts.

MESMER. Facts! Facts! Facts! You have a portfolio there stuffed with facts. Cripples, whom I've made to walk. Madmen, whom I've brought back to sanity. And you ask me how I did it. I tell you that there are forces in the human body so powerful and so mysterious that it may be centuries before they are fully understood. But the future historian will regard us as poor fools if we deny those forces, or fail to use them in the healing of mankind. (*To* LAMETTRIE.) You, Dr Lamettrie, are living in an age that you call—the Age of Reason. You look up to the sun, and you sneer at the light that comes from it. But you cannot prevent it from dazzling you. You look up to the moon and you say the moon is dead. But you cannot explain the mystery of its death. You look down to the earth, and you kick the clods with your contempt. But even as you kick it, that earth is vibrant with life, and light and energy.

Indeed, doctor, that clod of earth is radiating . . .

DR D'ESLON. What do you mean by radiating? (*Sarcastically*) Do you mean 'shining'?

MESMER. I mean sending out power.

DR D'ESLON. What sort of power?

MESMER. The same power that flows from hidden streams into the fingers of the water-diviner. The same power that flows from my own fingers into the bodies of the sick.

DR BARTHE. Witchcraft!

MESMER. The same power that vibrates in a ray of moonlight . . .

DR BARTHE. Moonshine . . . moonshine!

MESMER. And the day will come . . . I swear it . . . when we shall be able to capture that moonlight, and filter it through a glass, and weigh it and measure it and learn its message! *

Such was Mesmer's plea—in almost literally his own words —some two hundred years ago. It was a classic exposition of the underlying principle of radiesthesia, and if I say that it deeply moved and impressed me I shall not, I hope, be accused of immodesty. For I did not invent it; I only recorded it.

My final qualification for trying to write this book, rushing in where even the most intrepid angels might well fear to tread, is perhaps the most valid of all. It is simply because I believe the subject to be of such importance that I cannot stop myself from writing it. The whole world is suffering from a hardening of the spiritual arteries, to a degree that

* That this day is not scientifically so remote is suggested in the chapter that follows, in the section headed 'The Meaning of Moonlight'.

has never before been witnessed in the body politic. Such 'religious revivals' as manifest themselves, from time to time, flicker more and more feebly in the shadow of the atom bomb. If men are ever to be brought back to a more spiritual way of thinking I do not believe that it will be through any conventional 'religious revival' but through a general realization of the truths of radiesthesia. Those of us who express the hope that there may be such a general realization are not trying to revive the dusty and artificial conflict between science and religion; we are merely asserting—though possibly in a less hackneyed manner—that there is not, or should not be, any such conflict at all. It is all summed up in the phrase from Michael Ash's book, which I have already quoted: 'This is the power which so filled Jesus that the very hem of his garment was *alive* with it.' The phrase becomes even more luminous when we recall the original story from the New Testament that inspired it.

And much people followed him and thronged him. And a certain woman who had an issue of blood twelve years, and had suffered many things of many physicians, and had spent all that she had, and was nothing bettered, but rather grew worse, when she had heard of Jesus, came in the press behind, and touched his garment.

For she said 'If I may touch but his clothes, I shall be whole.' And straightway the fountain of her blood was dried up, and she felt in her body that she was healed of that plague.

And Jesus, immediately knowing in himself that virtue had gone out of him, turned in the press, and said 'Who touched my clothes?' *

This astonishing story rings down the centuries like a chime of bells. It vibrates; it has the timbre of total truth. And it is as 'modern' as if it had been published in the latest issue of one of the few journals that occasionally recognize the existence of the radiesthetic force. The key phrase, of course, is *'knowing in himself that virtue had gone out of him'*. This is the 'virtue' that is always given by those with the radiesthetic faculty, and since it is indeed 'virtue' the giving of it, though it may be momentarily exhausting, actually replenishes the powers of those who give. This is clearly

* Mark v, 25-30.

illustrated in the sequel to the story we have just quoted. Hardly had Jesus finished speaking to the woman He had healed of the issue of blood than news was brought to Him telling Him that the twelve-year-old daughter of the ruler of the synagogue had died. Immediately, He made His way through the crowd and entered the ruler's house. 'Why make ye this ado?' He asked. 'Why weep? The damsel is not dead, but sleepeth.' And there and then He proceeded to work one of the greatest of all His miracles. Heaven must have been very near to earth on that unforgettable day, and a great light must have been shining through its gates.

I believe this light to be still shining if we would but open our eyes.

These, then, are the main reasons which have impelled me to write this book.

There is one more. It can be put very simply by saying that for the average man and woman even the smallest knowledge of radiesthesia will add very greatly to the excitement of life in general.

I repeat, *excitement*, meaning a stimulation of the perceptions, a widening of the horizons and a sharpening of the senses. The knowledge that our own bodies are the transmitters and receivers of an infinite network of 'radiations'— I shall be obliged to make plentiful use of that not altogether satisfactory word—is thrilling enough to rob even an empty room of its solitude. Or even a *picture* of an empty room. As one stares at one's reproduction of Van Gogh's *Yellow Chair* one feels that it is 'radiating', as it were, by proxy, and that the 'radiations' of the passion with which he invested this humble but immortal object are matching with one's own 'radiations', by some miraculous system of radiesthetic mathematics.* The knowledge that these vibrations are dancing

---

* One of the strange things about the writing of this book has been that constantly I have found myself setting down phrases of which I scarcely knew the meaning, only to have them confirmed and explained, shortly afterwards, by independent testimony. The mention of Van Gogh is a case in point. While the chapter was being typed the postman delivered a little magazine called *Grace*. Opening it at random I found an article entitled 'Healing Radiations from Pictures', by Mrs Kingsley Tarpey, claiming that certain pictures, even if they were centuries old, continued to emit *therapeutic radiations of a physical nature*, entirely apart from any psychological benefits which might be derived from the beauty

from the petals of a daffodil, and that the flowers themselves are aware of them, as they are aware of the errant attentions of the wind . . . all this enriches, to an infinite degree, one's interest in things that are green and growing. The knowledge that there is an affinity, or an antipathy, between a man and the soil he treads, and that these affinities or antipathies are 'radiating' around him, even if he cannot see them . . . this makes of even the dullest walk down the dreariest lane an enduring miracle. The marvel of life and the music of life are immeasurably enhanced by the study of radiesthesia. In even so simple a symbol as that of the hazel twig, as it twists and turns in the hands of the dowser, there is a miraculous rhythm. It is obeying the summons of hidden waters. It has heard a song from far below, a liquid music written on invisible staves. But the 'dead' twig has heard it . . . the 'dead' twig dances to it, dances to the music of the dark waters far below.

For such a theme one needs the pen of Blake. I own no such eminent instrument. Only a reporter's pencil. You will find the result of this reportage in the chapter that follows.

of their subject-matter. This claim was reinforced by the work of two scientists—Dr Oscar Brunler and Major F. A. Menaies—who spent a number of years gathering evidence that 'every painter imparts to his work his own *radiation signature;* an unmistakable, unchangeable radiation pattern that cannot be faked or imitated, or in any way tampered with, but remains a permanent pattern of authenticity.' If this claim could ever be substantiated there will have to be a considerable reshuffling in the world's art galleries.

3. THE MAGIC ROD

ACCIDENT 'BLACK SPOTS'
SCIENTIST'S STARTLING CLAIM
RADIATION THEORY

I have chosen to begin this chapter with a slab of journalese because it is one way of keeping our feet on the ground. After several weeks spent in poring over one of the most difficult books* I have ever tried to digest, there has emerged a general picture of very great complexity—like an immense landscape which fades into mountains reaching to infinite skies. However, from this landscape certain homely details stand out which can at least be indicated to the general reader—as though a guide in an art gallery, who was not too sound on his aesthetics, were to point his finger to a horse or a tree or a church, and say his little piece about it.

Perhaps we should introduce the artist who painted the landscape—Professor Cecil Maby. Not even his detractors would deny that there is little to learn which Maby has not learnt about water-divining—or 'dowsing', a good old seventeenth-century word. (The fact that it *is* a seventeenth-century word is not, perhaps, without significance.) The list of his published works on this and kindred subjects is formidable, and represents the concentrated research of thirty years at an average of seventy hours a week. Unfortunately, the scientific terrain of dowsing in this country is loosely defined, and sometimes, studying the claims and counter-claims of the various contestants, one is reminded of a group of ex-

* *The Physics of the Divining Rod*. Being an account of an experimental investigation of water and mineral divining by J. Cecil Maby, B.SC., A.R.C.S., F.R.A.S. and T. Bedford Franklin, M.A., F.R.S.E. Published by George Bell & Sons Ltd, 1939.

plorers from rival countries squabbling over the correct ap-
portionment of an uncharted jungle. It has been Maby's life-
work to map out that jungle and to define its scientific limitations. The reader will hardly be surprised to learn that it is
with some reluctance that he discusses these matters with
the untutored. However, he has a kindly tolerance for those
who he feels are at least *trying* to understand his findings.

But we were talking about Accident Black Spots. These
emerged during a comparatively light-hearted interlude in
our conversation. Maby's mind is so pervaded by radionics—
which is a very different thing from saying that he is obsessed
by them—that he is able to perceive their application in
situations where they have not hitherto been suspected. In
this case he concluded that the constant recurrence of accidents at certain places in which no special element of danger was apparent might well be due to the presence of
a strong undercurrent of water. To put it very simply, the
arm of a tired lorry driver, as he passed over this hidden
stream, would be subjected to an invisible 'tug'.

This conclusion he has since proved, by painstaking experiment, with a degree of certainty that would satisfy any
British jury.

(When I told him that this was a front-page news story
he blinked and said, 'Indeed?' Professor Maby, bless his
heart, has no very strongly developed sense of journalistic
values—not that journalistic values are invariably contemptible.)

Let us return to that word 'tug', and illustrate it by a story.
A while ago Maby was doing a job of professional dowsing
in a rural district. He can read these hidden streams, which
flow through our lives with a greater potency for good or
evil than most of us have guessed, with an uncanny facility.
He found that this particular stream led him to the village
forge, and conducted directly under the anvil. A couple of
men were working at this anvil, sweating away with their
hammers, as their forefathers had done for centuries before
them. He put away his dowsing rod for a moment.

'Would you chaps like me to tell you how to make your
work a good deal easier?'

The chaps grunted a suitable reply.

'All you have to do is to move this anvil over to the corner.
And then . . .'

And then, I fear, the Professor may have become a little

too technical for the chaps. He may have begun to chat lightly about the *'parallel zones of reaction in the primary radiation field, due to serialised rotations of the plane of polarisation and also the transverse waves of increasing and decreasing field strength (non-polarised effect) due to the secondary induction field'*. (Which is the sort of thing that this distracted author has been trying to grapple with for the past six months.)

Anyway, they did not move the anvil. They preferred to go on sweating, rather than listen to the meanderings of an obviously insane professor. There may be a moral in this story. There may be many men in the world using a great deal of unnecesssary energy over anvils of all sorts . . . energy which might be saved by learning some of the lessons of the divining rod.

The homely example of the anvil was chosen not only because it helps to 'keep our feet on the ground', but also because it serves to emphasize the fact that Maby's main task in the long course of his investigations has been to prove the *physical* faculty of dowsing. He does not concern himself with the *psychical* faculty, as exemplified by such phenomena as map-dowsing, nor the tracing of lost persons and corpses; equally he does not dismiss these practices as necessarily bogus. Indeed, he keeps rather more than an open mind about it, admitting that it seems 'highly probable' that in some cases—the sort of cases which we shall be examining later —'a cryptopsychic faculty may be utilised'. This admission, from a man whose mind is so antiseptically guarded against deceit, illusion, and all that is not capable of scientific proof, seems of importance. However, at this point, what concerns us is his emphatic conclusion—which has never been seriously contested*—that the reaction of the dowser is as plainly

* Perhaps it would be more accurate to say *convincingly* contested. Even some of those who are most eager for the acceptance of radionics into respectable scientific society seem at times confused about it. Thus J. O. Wilcox, in his recent book *Radionics* (Jenkins, London 1960), postulates the theory that the dowser projects a 'thought form', and that this form 'unites in some way with the water radiations'. And he concludes that 'if there is no water, his thought form finds, as it were, no target, and there is consequently no response from the instrument.' An hour spent in Maby's laboratories would, one hopes, dispel such illusions.

physical as the reaction of the electric light bulb when we turn on the switch.

To put it in his own words:

> We think we may claim incontrovertibly to have shown that the causes of the ordinary dowsing reflexes and rod reactions are to be found in *certain penetrating, electrically excitory rays:* one class—the more important of the two—consisting of short Hertzian waves of geo-physical or cosmic origin, and exhibiting polarisation and electro-magnetic phenomena.

The average reader may find it necessary to read that sentence again. But it is not really so obscure. In a later chapter we shall find these 'rays' masquerading under all sorts of different names and strange disguises, some of them of great dramatic interest. Meanwhile it is enough to remind ourselves that they *exist* . . . that they are all around us, everywhere, all the time.

Perhaps it is time to dip our pen once more in the journalistic inkpot. We might do this by means of our obliging 'tug'. In other and lighter moments Maby has experimented with numerous examples of this 'tug'. So let us assume that he is dowsing a field, and that he finds water running at a depth of 200 feet in, say, the north-east corner. To mark the site of this hidden stream he drives a peg into the soil. He walks to the other three corners—where there is *no* water—and drives in similar pegs. He then strolls round to the pub, contacts an unsuspecting young man, and inveigles him back to the field 'for a little experiment'. He thrusts a crowbar into the young man's hand, and leads him to the pegs in the various corners, keeping the north-east to the last. At each peg he requests the young man to lift the crowbar at arm's length—a feat which he performs with no difficulty at all. But at the fourth corner something seems to go wrong: the crowbar has suddenly become unaccountably heavier, and the young man sweats and strains as he lifts it. Odd, he thinks, that he should tire so quickly. But his condition has nothing to do with fatigue; it is the work of the aforesaid 'short Hertzian waves of geophysical or cosmic origin', exercising a 'tug' which may in some instances be equivalent to a thirty per cent depreciation of muscular energy.

One wonders how Mr. Wilcox, with his theory of 'thought forms', would explain this simple experiment, which Maby

has tested again and again? Our young man with the crowbar was not concerning himself with 'thought form' or 'radiations'. If he had any 'thought forms' at all they were probably directed towards a second pint of beer at the pub. His
reaction was an objective reaction obtained in the absence of
any bystanders, and without any mental suggestion.

Such cases, obviously, in the hands of an unscrupulous
journalist, could be distorted and headlined, and cause Maby
no little embarrassment. The atmosphere in which he works
is the rarified atmosphere of pure science, and only occasionally does he descend to the pavement level of the man in
the street, bearing with him these strangely fascinating examples of the rays at their ceaseless work.

All the same, there is nothing intrinsically base about headlines; truth is truth in whatever type you print it, and simply
because these truths are so important I shall ask the com-
positors to reach, once more, for capital letters.

OLYMPIC SENSATION
WHO WON THE HIGH JUMP?
RUSSIANS BLAME HOSTILE RAYS

Forgive me, Professor . . . you really asked for it. These
rare descents into my sort of terrain, from the heights which
you normally inhabit, are an irresistible temptation to the
journalist . . . or indeed, to the dramatist or to the poet. To
prove my good intentions, let us quote one of the last paragraphs from your formidable work, in which, at the end of
your long journey, you seem to push aside your mass of data,
to relax, to allow yourself a smile, and to write:

Changes of field strength and polar reversals may also
alter the conditions between two competitors' individual
attempts, absurd as that may appear. So that it looks as
though dowsers may one day find themselves with yet
another occupation, viz. selecting neutral sites for sports
grounds, stages and other arenas.

Nor is it drawing the long-bow to suggest that acro-
bats and jugglers, who have to perform strenuous and
skilful feats that involve balancing and a variety of precise movements of a muscular kind, will likewise be considerably affected. In fact, local conditions and sudden
changes of field strength or polarity may well be held
responsible for the otherwise unaccountable failures of

tricks and feats that have been performed successfully a thousand times before, even though the exhibitor should happen to be free from 'nerves', and perfectly fit and in practice. For strong dowsing radiation makes the muscles inclined to tremble under strain, and balancing becomes unusually hard to achieve. We have most of us, at one time or another, noticed such sporadic variations of our strength and skill, and may have attributed them to incompetence, ill-health or fatigue. Here, however, we find ourselves at last confronted with another and surer explanation; and a pretty fly in the ointment of sporting trials it seems to be! *

I may be giving the impression that to Maby, and to the very few living men who can hope to rival his erudition and share his vision, dowsing might be an almost aridly academic process, which would be more suitably entrusted to a machine. And it is indeed true that he does envisage the day when some form of mechanical device will supplant the dowser's fingers. As he said to me:

'The human dowser reacts to so many forms of outside interference that sometimes it is difficult, if not impossible, to sort them out. He reacts to radio waves, to gamma waves; he reacts to ultra-violet waves; he may even be affected by walking out of the sunlight into the deep shadow of a tree.'

All these reactions, of course, are physical.

And—here we come to one of those paradoxes by which the whole problem is beset—even human emotional excitement is physically 'translated'. Before he raps me over the fingers for putting it in that way let me shelter behind one of his own illustrations.

'Supposing', he said, 'that a woman is sitting near me while I'm doing my stuff. And supposing that she suddenly opens a telegram telling her that her son has been killed. What happens? Because of the intense emotional shock which she has just received, *she bumps the ether*. The resultant surrounding electric disturbance can, in fact, be detected by dowsing and by suitable automatic instruments.'

That is something that all of us can understand—one little fragment of the puzzle that we can fit into place. Like so many of Maby's observations it illuminates a far wider screen than that to which it is immediately directed. Thus, although

* *Physics of the Divining Rod*, p. 472.

one has heard a great deal about 'crowd psychology' it has never, as far as I am aware, been explained in terms of 'etheric bumps'. Perhaps it might be more fruitful if the guardians of our civil defence were to pay rather more attention to these than to the more prosaic bumps on the head.

However, all these kinds of examples, even if they could be given a 'psychic twist' by the ardent spiritualist, are—so Maby insists—purely *physical*. He does not deny that in some spheres of radiesthesia the psychic and physical territories appear to overlap. That is not his primary concern; he stays strictly on the more objective side of the border. When at the end of a very difficult conversation I quoted to him Edison's wish that his last and greatest invention might be to fashion a substance so sensitive that it might be affected by thought, he replied drily, 'Not thought itself. There would have to be some physical concomitant, which would be mainly due to an electro-chemical disturbance of the nerves and other tissues.' He added that changes of this nature could already be detected by an instrument on which I am quite unqualified to comment—the electroencephalograph.

Later, we shall be learning that Edison's wish has—at least in some people's opinion—come very near to being realized in the Delawarr Laboratories at Oxford. But there is a lot of ground to be covered before we can even begin to consider such claims.

I can only hope to continue groping through the scientific jungle—which is made all the more intimidating by the fact that owing to its proximity to psychic territories it is lit by a 'light that never was, on sea or land'—if I continue to clutch tightly to the reporter's notebook, jotting down a headline as it suggests itself and seeing whether, under this headline, I can write a few words to illuminate it.

Let us begin at random with:

THE FATAL BEDSTEAD

This was suggested by Chapter VIII of Maby's book which is concerned with 'Electric Radiations relative to Growth and Disease'. This chapter owes something to the researches, among others, of a French engineer named Lakhovsky, who did much to stimulate interest in the question of certain:

NOXIOUS TERRESTRIAL RAYS

He claims that these rays were a factor in aggravating cancer and, in all probability, a number of other diseases such as asthma, tuberculosis and rheumatism in its various guises. To say that Maby accepts this claim as conclusively proved would be to go too far, but he regards it as a 'valuable working hypothesis'. He also seems to think it not impossible that Lakhovsky was 'on to something' when he maintained that 'these noxious rays could be "screened away"' from human beings by means of certain neutralizing devices. And in this connection he quotes the work of another French scientist, Labergerie, and his researches on the effects of copper when worn in close and constant contact with the human skin. To many superior persons the copper bracelet is a 'gadget', a social toy, a badge of childish superstition. Labergerie did not think so, and produced an impressive amount of evidence in support of the 'super activation effect on rheumatic and neuralgic conditions'. This effect was due to the 'ionization* of the air in the magnetic field induced by the metallic oscillators'. So it would seem that the wearing of copper bracelets—a habit which, incidentally, can be traced back to ancient Egypt—is not quite so foolish after all. As for the 'ionization fields'—which is only another way of saying the areas in the immediate vicinity of the copper—that these actually *exist* has been proved by Maby with a certainty that admits of no contradiction. 'They are detectable and measurable', he states, 'by means of classical recording instruments.'

But our Fatal Bedstead is still waiting for us. Let us pause for breath, draw a line, and consider it in the next section.

Where have we got so far? By a series of short cuts, which are admittedly ludicrous in so long and tortuous a journey, we have recognized—through the medium of dowsing—the existence of certain penetrating, electrically excitory rays, of which the most important class are short Hertzian waves of

---

* One of the definitions of an 'ion' in the Oxford Dictionary is 'a gaseous particle electrically charged', and of 'ionization'—'the production of ions in a gas, so making it a conductor'. It is interesting to note that thunderclouds are strongly 'ionized' which is, of course, the reason why dowsers find it difficult to work in thundery weather.

geophysical or cosmic origin. These are the rays that cause the rod to move in the dowser's hands. The movement, it should be noted, seems always upwards or downwards, with no particular factor causing it to choose one direction or the other. I have never heard of a rod moving sideways.

We have also encountered certain 'noxious terrestrial rays', with effects that appear to be inimical to health, thanks to their disruptive and ionizing capacity. And though these rays may be normally so penetrative as to pass harmlessly through the human body, there are many circumstances—natural and artificial—which charge them, as it were, with malignancy. In nature the increased 'bombardment' of these rays may be caused by underground streams and certain deposits, in which case people living near them are, in effect, being subjected to continuous treatment akin to a weak radium or X-ray therapy—the ultimate results of which may, of course, be irritating, depressing, or even fatal. The *artificial* enhancement of these rays and electric fields is due to the presence of metal of various kinds and in various quantities.

Two questions posed by Maby sum up this aspect of the situation:

Is it not possible that the increase of such complaints as cancer, tuberculosis and the rheumatic maladies may be partly due to (1) *the great increase of metal-work* in modern buildings, cars, factories, etc., as compared with more wood, brick, and stone in the past; and (2) *to the number of bungalow dwellers,* who sleep as well as work near ground level, where scattered radiation is appreciably stronger than upstairs or with intervening cellars? *

And now, at last, to our bedstead! He writes:

The effect on sensitive subjects of modern beds with iron frames, and massed coiled-steel spring mattresses immediately beneath their backs all night long, is a serious consideration. In one case of ours a sensitive subject's disturbed sleep and marked sensation of chilling, tingling, and cramp on one side of a metal bed was traced to some *radioactive inclusion in the latter, emit-*

* *Physics of the Divining Rod,* p. 374.

ting relatively intense corpuscular radiation at close quar-
ters. Health as well as sleep was adversely affected and
such a bedstead might have fatal consequences in some
cases.†

We suggested in Chapter Two that even a superficial knowledge of radionics made life more exciting. We may now be pardoned for suggesting that in some aspects of our 'civilization' it also makes life more alarming!

The reader will by now have realized that the 'magic rod' has purposes far wider than the sinking of a well in a village field. He will also have realized—even though we have only quoted a small fraction of the evidence—that in the streams which it discovers there may be potencies of far greater omen than can be illustrated by the simple picture of water running from a bathroom tap, and that some of these potencies may be malignant, since the streams so evidently act as channels of radioactivity. Again, he will have appreciated that the word 'dowsing', when it is spoken by a man of Maby's authority, has an almost infinite range, and that the 'rays' which the dowser detects, or tries to detect, have many names, many qualities, and many manifestations.

Finally, he will have realized that the whole science of radiesthesia lies in territory which it is difficult to define with absolute accuracy, since it is bordered by the vast and misty continent of the psychic. And from the mountains of this continent, as it were, there is a constant drift of cloud which tends to obscure the facts and hinder research. This point was neatly summed up in Maby's concluding address to a Technical Congress of Radionics recently held in London. He said:

It cannot be denied that the more subtle aspects of radiesthesia often abut upon, or even fuse with, certain phenomena of extra-sensory perception—clairvoyance, psychometry, 'etheric' projection etc. If so, it is right that radiesthetists should interest themselves in these matters, just as parapsychologists should interest themselves in some of the subtler aspects of radiesthesia. But we must be careful not to confuse the two issues, which, in their extremes, remain irreconcilable.

We will endeavour not to confuse these two issues. But since the reader, by now, will almost certainly feel that he

has earned the right to a little relaxation, we might conclude
this chapter by paying a visit to some of these border territories, while trying not to lose our way in the shadow of the
aforesaid 'psychic clouds'.

Noxious Rays and States of Mind. Practically every person of
sensitivity has noticed, at one time or another in his life, that
a certain house or locality 'gives him the creeps'. This feeling
—which is as definite as the sensations of heat and cold—
need not be due to any 'weirdness' in the atmosphere, nor
certainly to any ugliness in the surroundings; the house may
be brand new and the landscape may be beautiful. And yet
—he has 'the creeps'.

That this mental reaction—which after all is a *fact*—may
be sustained and, as it were, 'kept alive' by some sort of
radionic process—whatever the original cause of it—was
suggested to me by a radiesthetist who prefers to remain
anonymous. I met him shortly after I had returned from a
motoring trip to Land's End in Cornwall.

'By the way,' he said to me, 'when you were on your way
down, did you pass through any area in which you had a feeling of depression? I don't mean merely an ugly town or a
sprawling suburb, but a definite sensation of mental malaise?'

'I certainly did,' I answered. 'And I always do in that place.
It was when . . .'

He held up his hand. 'Don't tell me till I've written it down
on a piece of paper. Afterwards, we'll see if I was right.'

When he had written it down I told him that a few miles
outside Launceston, after crossing the little river Inney, I
reached a stretch of open country where, although the sun
was shining brightly, there was an unaccountable sensation
that the skies were darkening and that the air was chill. At a
bend in the road I was 'thumbed' by two women hikers with
packs on their backs. They looked so distressed that I pulled
up for them and opened the door. As they got in they both
sighed, as with one voice, 'Thank heavens!' And then the
elder woman said, 'This place was getting on our nerves.'
And the other said, 'Yes, it was giving us the creeps. I wonder
what it's called?'

I told them that it was called Bodmin Moor, and that it
gave me the creeps too. So much so that I hoped they would
not mind if I stepped on the gas.

When I had told this little story my friend unfolded his
piece of paper. On it he had written . . . Bodmin Moor.

The sceptic may tell me that Bodmin Moor might well de-

press anybody, because it is so bleak and desolate. But I have
a great fondness for the bleak and desolate; on the lonely
moors which Emily Brontë loved, my heart sings; I feel happy
in the heart of the fen country, when the world is hushed in
the falling dusk. This feeling about Bodmin Moor—which
was so strong during the war that it caused a disciplinary
crisis among troops who were quartered there—was something totally different.

Is it therefore so foolish to accept the radiesthetic explanation, as expounded by my friend?

Maybe we should call it 'radiesthesia plus', because although my friend agreed with Maby's general theories about
noxious rays and states of mind, he insisted that at some time
or other in the history of the moor some other element must
have been involved, a human element, presumably of a tragic
or evil nature, which had (in Maby's own phrase) 'bumped
the ether' and was still 'bumping it', still using these rays as
a means for transmitting a message powerful enough to de-
press the spirits of those sensitive enough to receive it.

A single sentence from one of the most remarkable books
I have ever read—*The Imprisoned Splendour**—can perhaps
give us a short cut to some sort of understanding of this
theme, with its infinite implications. In discussing the phenomenon of man's memory Dr Johnson observes:

> We tend to assume, because of our familiarity with
> our own mental functioning, that the mind alone has
> memory. In fact we may have to admit that something
> akin to memory (i.e. some kind of record) exists on
> every level (physical and mental); that even inanimate
> matter may have its own memory akin to that passive
> habit-type associated with our brains, and that the 'psy-
> chic ether' which we have postulated may be the vehicle
> of such a record or memory.

After noting that if objects have this type of cognizable
memory, so have places and buildings, and reminding us
that psychical research has provided much evidence to the
effect that this memory can apparently be tapped, he crystal-

* *The Imprisoned Splendour*. An Approach to Reality, based upon
the significance of data drawn from the fields of Natural Science,
Psychical Research, and Mystical Experience by Raynor C. Johnson, M.A. (Oxon.), PH. D., Master of Queen's College, University
of Melbourne. Published by Hodder & Stoughton, 1953.

lizes this speculation in one unforgettable phrase: *Rocks cannot remember, but they may hold a memory which the mind of man in favourable circumstances can cognize.*

In such a theme Wordsworth might have heard echoes which would have deepened and enriched his intimations of immortality.

So much then for our 'radiesthetic explanation' of the mystery of Bodmin Moor. Like so many other 'explanations' it is half in one world and half in another, which is why I sometimes feel that this book is being written by moonlight.

However, to write by moonlight is not necessarily to write moonshine, as I hope to prove in the next section.

The Meaning of Moonlight. I have often been puzzled by the apparent comtempt of some scientists for *words—qua* words: for their inability to realize that a word that has stood up to the test of time is, in itself, a testimony to an historical fact—to a whole accumulation of historical facts, in the same way that an ancient coin is testimony to a whole series of commercial transactions. Indeed, the witness of the word is perhaps more trustworthy than the witness of the coin, for the coin may be debased or lose its value, whereas the word remains in circulation and usually keeps much of its original significance.

Consider the word 'lunatic'—a word which has a ring of truth across whatever argumentative counter it may be thrown. It derives—one need scarcely remind the reader!—from the Latin *luna*, meaning the moon, and from the age-old superstition that madmen are affected by the moon's waxing and waning. If you were to express a belief in this superstition to any of those who are in charge of our mental institutions—as certain friends of mine have actually done—you would almost certainly be greeted with derision . . . and perhaps not surprisingly; these harassed officials have quite enough to distract them without worrying about what the moon is up to. And yet the very fact that a superstition *is* age-old should surely entitle it to some respect? Smoke that blows from such distant places, across so many faded pages of history, must surely indicate the presence, somewhere, of a fire, even if it is a pale-flamed fire, lit from far above.

Radionics seem to confirm the existence of this strange kindling. The moon is a magnet—not comparable with the immensely powerful magnet of the earth, with its solid iron core—but a magnet none the less. And there is much evidence to suggest that the moon, thanks to its effects on the atmosphere and the electro-magnetic fields—effects which are *measurable*—may affect not only dowsers and geophysical instruments, but also the unbalanced nervous systems of 'mental' subjects, whether they are inside an asylum or—as is more often—outside it. One might say that not only does it twist the rod in the dowser's hands, but it also distorts the images in the madman's brain.*

But not all the results of moonlight are malignant. Among peasant folk the world over, there is an ancient and persistent tradition that the moon has a marked effect on the growth of plants. In this age of artificial fertilizers and synthetic poisons the idea that the rays of the moon may conceivably be more potent then something which comes out of a packet may seem positively archaic. And yet to quote Maby again: 'Many expert gardeners (two known to the writer) always plant by the moon, and they certainly get particularly good results.' And Madame Kolisko, author of *The Moon and the Growth of Plants*† has published a series of remarkable photographs to prove her claim that *all* plant growths are stimulated to a healthier reaction and a more permanent virility if they are sown *two days before full moon*. As an insatiable journalist I would like to be able to substantiate this claim; as an overworked gardener I regret that I cannot do so. I have only a cold greenhouse, and a gardener—admittedly a brilliant one—who comes two days a week. If we were to start experiments by moonlight I should have to pay a great deal of overtime, and I doubt whether the results would justify the expenditure.

* Maby and several other workers in this field consider that there is an even stronger influence in the 11½-year solar (sunspot) cycle, which seems clearly to affect many classes of vital phenomena—meteorology, plant growth, and even human industrial productivity. Statistical support for these claims is to be found in surprising places, such as the records of the Stock Exchange.
† Anthroposophical Publishing Co., 1939.

4. BABEL

Meditating among liars, and retreating sternly into myself,
I see that there are really no liars after all,
And nothing fails its perfect return—And that what are
                    called lies are perfect returns
And that each thing exactly represents itself, and what
                    has preceded it
And that the truth includes all
And henceforth I will go celebrate anything I see or am
And sing and laugh and deny nothing.

                                        WALT WHITMAN

If I were reading this book, instead of writing it, I suspect that I might already have some cause for complaint.

Laying it aside for a moment, I should address the author along these lines:

'You have written much about a mysterious "force" but you have not really told us what it *is*. And though you have suggested that it may have considerable potencies for good or evil, the examples you have given, so far, are not strong enough to inspire me with hope nor fill me with alarm.

'But my most serious objection is that you do not seem to have made up your mind as to whether the "force" is physical or psychic. In Chapter One—where you report your visit to Dr Ash—you appear to suggest that it is entirely psychic, or, if you prefer the word, "spiritual". You tell us that the power from his hands caused your body to react in a manner that could not have been induced by any normal physical or mechanical processes. (Incidentally, even in this example, which I am prepared to accept, you omitted to inform us whether the treatment did you any good!) * But in Chapter Three—where you ask us to follow you in your long dissertation on the divining rod—you appear to come down entirely on the side of the physical. You attribute all these phenomena to . . . what was it? . . . "certain penetrating, electrically excitory rays" which are being thrown off not only by underground streams but by metals and other physical objects—even by the material faculties of moonlight. In these statements also, being an amiable reader, I am prepared to give you the benefit of the doubt, not only be-

---

* It was completely and permanently successful. B.N.

cause Professor Maby's findings are presumably open to investigation but because it is common knowledge that water-diviners are widely employed in commercial undertakings.

'But I do not see how you can have it both ways. If Dr Ash's powers are psychic, are you trying to tell us—to take a rather ludicrous example—that they would not work if he were in close proximity to one of these underground streams? If—to take another rather ludicrous example—the effect of moonlight on the brain of a lunatic is indeed malignant, by what precise physical processes is this malignancy communicated?'

So my imaginary reader might phrase his complaints. And the fact that I have brought him on to the stage at all may make him suspect that I am learning my job in public . . . that I am writing this book 'as I go along'.

In this suspicion he would be correct. I *am* writing this book 'as I go along', for the simple reason that I do not know how else it is to be written. And at this stage of our journey it is quite true that in our consideration of the X Force there appears to be an inextricable confusion between the physical and the psychic.

That phrase—'the X Force'—is in itself a confession of the improvisatory nature of our inquiry. It might quite as well have been 'the vital force' or 'the unknown power' or a dozen other phrases with which one attempts to pin down the unpinnable. However, we will let it stand.

How are we to resolve this confusion? Perhaps our best plan would be to call a few of those many distinguished witnesses who, throughout history, have testified to—at least—the *existence* of this force. What did they say about it? How did they describe its qualities and assess its potentialities?

And what name did they give it?

What name! We may well ask this question, though we shall not find it so easy to answer.

For one of the principal stumbling blocks confronting the student of radiesthesia, at the outset of his inquiries, is this problem of nomenclature. Time and again he encounters the same mysterious force masquerading under a different name. At first this multiplicity of titles is not only baffling but irritating; little by little, however, the irritation is replaced by a feeling of curiosity, indeed, of awe. So many men—none of them fools—making the same discovery and, because they had arrived at it by independent routes, inventing a new set of terms with which to announce it to the world. It is rather as though successive groups of explorers had all ventured into an uncharted continent with the object of arriving at the centre. And having all been guided to precisely the same place, by means which they scarcely understood, proceeded to hoist their flags and annex it in the name of science, without realizing that it had already been annexed by many men who had come before.

The ensuing paragraphs owe a great debt to the researches of one of the most tireless workers in this field, Dr Aubrey Westlake, whose book *The Pattern of Health* is compulsory reading for every student. We shall be paying a personal visit to this retiring genius in the next chapter. In the meantime we could have no better guide than Dr Westlake to introduce us to a few of the pioneers. He names:

Paracelsus (1490-1541). This famous—or some would say notorious—medieval physician 'regarded the healing process of nature as a sort of magnetic influence or force, and he believed that everybody possessing it could arrest or heal disease in others'.* In Paracelsus' own words 'the vital force is not enclosed in man but radiates in and around him *like a luminous sphere and it may be made to act at a distance*. It may poison the essence of life [blood] and cause disease, or it may purify it and restore the health.' Paracelsus gave to this force the name of

MUNIA

Van Helmont (1577-1644). Like Paracelsus he postulated a 'secret property enabling one person to affect another . . . not a physical substance which we measure or weigh, but *an ethereal spirit, pure living, which pervades all things*.' To the means by which this secret property worked he gave the name of

MAGNALE MAGNUM

Anton Mesmer (1734-98). This erratic genius—the bridge between the medieval alchemists and the psychotherapists of the modern world—gave to the vital force yet another name:

* Sir William Osler, *The Evolution of Modern Medicine* (Yale University Press, 1921).

ANIMAL MAGNETISM

Christian Scientists will hardly need to be reminded that to Mary Baker Eddy, a century later, 'animal magnetism' became more and more synonymous with the work of the Devil. So much so that she could never speak or write of it without the prefix 'malicious'. To the sceptic, Mrs Eddy's 'malicious animal magnetism' has been the subject of much contemptuous comment, but was she so wrong after all? Paracelsus would not have thought so. His 'munia', we must remember, could not only restore health but 'poison the essence of life'.

We may mention one other important point about Mesmer before we pass on. Although the term 'animal magnetism' is now no longer current in radiesthetic circles, all the later workers in this field accepted his claim that the human body has 'polarity' and other properties analogous to a magnet. The homeliest example of this is to be found in the popular notion that it is best to sleep with one's head to the magnetic north.

I may mention—if only to give us a moment's light relief—that the first person who ever introduced me to this theory, a long time ago, was the Edwardian novelist Elinor Glyn, whose *Three Weeks* was the *Lady Chatterley* of my prep school days. It was at a cocktail party in New York, and after she had propounded her ideas she applied them to our hostess. 'I am quite sure', she said, 'that the reason poor Millicent is so neurotic and tense is because she is sleeping improperly.' There were perhaps other interpretations of the impropriety of Millicent's sleeping habits, but Mrs Glyn was referring only to her 'magnetic maladjustment' and in order to prove it she conducted me to the bedroom, where people were leaving their hats and coats. 'You see,' she exclaimed, pointing dramatically to the bed, 'it is as I thought. The pillows point due east!' I asked her how she could tell without a magnet. 'Because I *am* a magnet,' she retorted. 'If I were sleeping in this room I should automatically move the bed at an angle of forty-five degrees to the window.' I was so interested in this bizarre conception that I later took the trouble to check it. Mrs Glyn's built-in magnet proved to be dead on the mark.

Dr D'Eslon (1764-1832). As D'Eslon was Mesmer's most devoted disciple he did not alter the name of the 'vital force', but he condensed and clarified its properties in a classic formulation of its laws. Some of these properties are worth remembering, because we find them cropping up again and again in the work of later pioneers. Thus, after describing animal magnetism as a 'universal, continuous fluid, constituting an absolute plenum in nature' he goes on to observe that *'it can operate at a great distance, without the intervention of any body.'*

This immediately throws a brilliant and not unkindly light on the work of contemporary 'spiritual healers', whose claims to perform miracles by 'absent healing' might otherwise strike us as incredible.

An even more remarkable property of animal magnetism, according to D'Eslon, is that it can be *'concentrated, accumulated and stored'*.

Here the reader may forgive me if we refer again to the story about Bodmin Moor in the previous chapter, in which we quoted the striking phrase of Dr Raynor Johnson: *'Rocks cannot remember, but they may hold a memory which the mind of man in favourable circumstances can cognize.'*

Surely this is only a dramatic presentation of the Mesmeric theory as propounded by D'Eslon and those who came after him?

I was so enthralled by the implications of this conception, this 'storing' business, this accumulation of energy in apparently inanimate objects, that I was bold enough to write to Dr Johnson to ask if he could throw further light on the subject. He was good enough to reply at length in a letter of which the greater part is so far above the general level of these pages—which are intended for comparatively painless consumption—that we will not quote it. The relevant portion, about the rocks, is prefaced by the following observation:

> I feel strongly that the *mental* level with its vast extensions is the basic level of *causes,* and the *physical* level to which our senses respond is largely a level of *effects.* It is becoming clearer and clearer to me that mind and matter are not at all contrasting elements in the world's structure, but rather that we have to deal with *one* reality which it is convenient to regard as 'stratified'.

Pursuing the metaphor of 'stratification' he suggests that the upper levels of this one reality are 'mind-like', that the lower levels are 'matter-like', and that between these two extremes there is a large range of levels containing these two kinds of qualities in different proportions. This, he points out, is the region of psychical or occult phenomena.

And now to the rocks:

> There is, I think, no such thing as *mere* matter. All physical objects are a 'precipitate' from the level of mind and therefore carry with them always what might be described as a 'mental field'. As soon as we recognize this, we are able to say that a so-called physical object retains a 'memory' or at least a 'record' of its experience and of its history, and that this 'record' would be identified by the higher quality of mind which we find in human beings.

Since I did not write it I can, without presumption, suggest that the reader studies this passage again, and even again, until he has thoroughly grasped its implications. For these are, indeed, awe-inspiring. If they are true, thousands of ghost stories will have to be moved to a new department of the national libraries. They will no longer be classified under Fiction; they will belong to the realm of Fact.

With the passing of the nineteenth century the list of investigators of this 'vital force', this mysterious 'magnetism', this 'fluid' multiplies exceedingly. And so, alas, do the number of names by which it is described. Of all these, perhaps the most significant and comprehensive was the word

ODYLE*

Baron Carl von Reichenbach was the originator of this title. Those who, like myself, have small knowledge of scientific history, may need to be reminded that he was one of the most eminent scientists of the nineteenth century whose *Researches*† made him famous in every civilized country, even if the fame later soured into notoriety. He was certainly no fly-by-night, and so little of a dreamer that some of his discoveries—such as creosote—have become essential to modern industry as we know it today.

* The term is derived from the Norse deity Odin, signifying 'a power penetrating all nature'.
† The full title is *Researches on Magnetism, Electricity, Light, Crystallization and Chemical Attraction in their Relation to the Vital Force* (Walton, 1853).

With Reichenbach's odyle the 'vital force' expands, as it were, into infinity—he sees it as 'interpenetrating and filling the structure of the universe'. And yet, if we carefully study his conclusions, we see that it was the same force noted by Paracelsus, the same mysterious 'fluid'—he even speaks of it 'flowing'—which formed the raw material of Mesmer's therapy.

And now we are beginning to recognize certain familiar features of this mystery, by whatever name we may call it. Here are some of the properties of odyle, as Reichenbach describes it:

1. It is radiated to great distances, the rays 'penetrating through such substances as clothes and brick walls'. (Compare the phenomenon of 'absent healing'.)

2. It can be *stored,* and substances can be charged with it.

3. It has polarity. This was already generally accepted, but Reichenbach carried it further by stating that there is negative odyle, which gives a sensation of coolness and is pleasant, and positive odyle, which gives a sensation of warmth and discomfort.

4. It is luminous.

And with this word 'luminous' we come to the most startling of Reichenbach's contentions, which was probably one of the principal reasons why he incurred the odium of his scientific contemporaries. *He stated that all human beings are containers of odyle; and all human beings are luminous over the whole surface.*

In Reichenbach's day psychical research was still in its infancy, which is presumably why his contemporaries found the conception of luminosity hard to digest. Today there is so much evidence for it—usually in the shape of an 'aura' encircling the head—that unless tens of thousands of men, women and children all over the world are blatant frauds, unanimously telling the same lie in the same imagery—with seldom any profit motive—the 'aura' phenomenon must be accepted by all but the most purblind. We cheerfully give credence to many phenomena for which there is no comparable body of evidence.

As far as the luminosity of the human body is concerned, I have taken it for granted since early childhood. I was first introduced to it at the age of seven through the medium of my governess. She was as nearly a saint as any human being I have ever met. (A few readers of some earlier books of mine, beginning with *Down the Garden Path,** may remem-

* Cape, 1936.

ber her in the guise of 'Miss Hazlitt'.) One morning, at the beginning of our lessons, which were always prefaced by a reading from *Daily Light*, Miss Hazlitt showed me a coloured reproduction of a picture of St Francis walking through a forest with the birds fluttering round him and all sorts of endearing animals peering between the trunks of the trees, with very saintly expressions. But it was his halo that caught my attention.

'What is that funny thing round his head, Miss Hazlitt?'

'That is his halo.'

'What is a halo?'

Invented dialogue, in autobiography, can be very tiresome, so I will merely observe that she told me what it was. The next few moments, by a freak of memory, I recall clearly.

'Have I a halo, Miss Hazlitt?'

'Yes.'

'Is it made of gold?'

She smiled and shook her head.

I ran to the looking-glass.

'I can't see it. Is it a nice halo?'

'It is a very nice one.'

'If you can see it, why can't I see it?'

'We cannot see our own haloes.'

(This is apparently the universal experience of those psychics who have the gift of seeing auras. They can never see their own.)

A year or two later, shortly before Miss Hazlitt left us, she told me—rather diffidently, for she was modest to the point of self-effacement—that she had seen auras ever since she was a small child, and that it was only by accident that she had learned that to most people they were invisible. In the golden luminosity that encircles the heads of the saints she believed quite literally. There have been more foolish beliefs. Why should it be so ridiculous to suppose that a great artist, working in a state of spiritual exaltation, in an era of religious renaissance, should be given this particular revelation? If it *is* ridiculous, the scoffers have a great deal of explaining to do. They must produce some valid reason why thousands of great artists, working in total independence of one another, in many countries over many centuries, have apparently seen this luminosity so clearly that they have dipped their brushes into gold.

But Reichenbach was not 'an artist working in a state of spiritual exaltation', and if he dipped his brush in anything, he dipped it in creosote. Yet . . . he saw haloes too.

This chapter would be interminable were I to attempt to list all the men who found this same invisible 'vital force', experimented in their various ways with its powers—sometimes with tragic results—and proceeded to give it a different name, for the simple reason that they were working outside the recognized frontiers of science. But it is worth noting a few more of these names, if only to emphasize the fact that though the names become more and more diverse, the *thing* itself becomes more and more constant in its properties. At the risk of sounding perversely paradoxical one might say that these men, when they contemplated the invisible, were more and more certain what it looked like. And it always looked the same.

We will consider only two more names.

The first is

ORGONE

Dr Wilhelm Reich (1897-1957) who gave this name to the 'vital force' deserves a chapter to himself, and if one thing is certain in this uncertain world it is that I should be quite incapable of writing it. To do so one would need to have passed with first-class honours, as he did, in physiology, pathology, bacteriology, psychology, biology, cancer research, physics and meteorology, to mention only a few of the subjects in which he excelled.

Indeed, I am not even capable of giving an intelligent summary of his work, which carries us into realms far beyond the intellectual understanding of the layman. However, at least one can say that Reich, like all the others, found himself confronted by a 'force' to which he was obliged to give a new name . . . a force which is 'present everywhere, forming an uninterrupted continuum' . . . a force that 'penetrates everything' . . . a force that 'travels with the speed of light'.

This 'force' eventually killed him, as a result of experiments in which he was trying to tame it in accumulators of orgone energy, which he called 'orgonoscopes'. The whole history of these terrifying machines is difficult to disentangle, though an especially persistent student could presumably assemble the outlines of the picture by a study of the *Orgone Energy Bulletin,* a quarterly edited by Reich in the early 'fifties. Briefly, his aim was to set orgone energy 'fighting' atomic energy, on the theory that they were contradictory functions of nature and thus antagonistic to one another. In his efforts to do so he unleashed forces far greater than he had imagined. He summarized the conflict between these forces as follows:

Phase One. Nuclear energy affects orgone energy in a most damaging manner.

Phase Two. Orgone energy after the first blow fights back ferociously. It runs mad, runs berserk.

Phase Three. If orgone energy has the opportunity to keep fighting nuclear energy it will finally succeed in rendering it harmless. It will replace the noxious secondary activity of the nuclear energy by penetration of the nuclear energy matter and will put it at its service.*

All this, of course, sounds like science fiction at its most lurid. But it is not fiction, it is fact—one of the strangest episodes in American medical history. In 1947 the Federal Food and Drug Administration decided to 'investigate' Reich's mysterious machines, and indeed they had every reason to do so, for there were some very odd goings on in the neighbourhood of the Reich laboratories. In spite of every precaution against poisoning by atomic radiation—and Reich was eminently qualified to ensure that the precautions were adequate—workers were falling sick with alarming frequency; a power of unprecedented ferocity seemed to be generating itself, as though the fight between the two energies had developed in each of them a supernormal strength. To Reich, this was symbolic of their very natures; it was a fight between the primitive forces of good and evil. But he never had an opportunity of proving it. For in 1954 the Food and Drug Administration again intervened, and all his accumulators were ordered to be destroyed, on the remarkable grounds that 'orgone energy *does not exist*'. Two years later came the final blow. He was in the Arizona desert engaged on an experiment very near to his heart; an experiment in which he was employing this energy, this 'orgone', in the making of rain. And he was actually making it. According to a report of March 1955: 'What is being accomplished by Reich and his assistants in Arizona in combating the desert with Cosmic Orgone Engineering equals and excels the

* I am indebted for this summary to Dr Aubrey Westlake's *The Pattern of Health* (Vincent Stuart, 1961).

most optimistic theoretical anticipation.' But somebody in authority must have 'had it in' for Reich. In May 1956 he was arrested and sentenced to two years imprisonment. Eighteen months later he died, poisoned by the very 'orgone' which he had envisaged as a force for good—a force which he had stirred up to fight so fiercely that it struck and destroyed him.

One does not have to be endowed with supernatural insight to realize that in this narrative there is a great 'story', in the journalistic sense of the word, and maybe not only in the journalistic sense. For here was a man of formidable scientific accomplishment. That is on the record. Here was a man who was totally convinced of the existence of this same 'force'—'fluid', 'vibration', 'potency', 'radiation', call it what you will—that we have seen compelling the attention of pioneers since the days of Paracelsus. So convinced, indeed, that he gave his life in a vain endeavour to harness it. All this, too, is on the record.

Which suggests that in the proceedings of that revered body, the Food and Drug Administration of the United States, there might be a fruitful field for scientific research, if any scientist could be found who was brave enough, and rich enough—and crazy enough—to undertake it.

And now for our last name:

THE X FORCE

L. E. Eeman (1889-1958) who was responsible for our final definition of this mysterious Something which 'did not exist' was a well-known figure in London before the war. Indeed, his Baker Street consulting and treatment rooms were a sort of modern version of Mesmer's salon, with patients joining hands in co-operative healing. 'Joining hands' is perhaps an over-simplification of his techniques, for the patients were linked by means of copper wires held in both hands and connected with the spine and the back of the head. These were arranged in accordance with the body's polarity, and it is interesting to note that if the wires were reversed—negative to negative and positive to positive, instead of vice versa—the patients immediately experienced a feeling of acute tension instead of the customary relaxation. To this there is abundant testimony.

What was this 'something' that 'flowed' from hand to hand? What gave it this power to send a whole circle of

sick people to sleep . . . as it frequently did, and made them
feel afterwards, in Eeman's words, that 'each had got more
out of the pool than he had put into it'?

We seem to have asked that question before!

Most remarkable of all Eeman's experiments was his discovery that *drugs could be introduced into the circuit*. At
this point we obviously step into psychical territory—if we
have not been there all along—and I shall not attempt an
explanation of this phenomenon until we have covered more
ground. But in the meantime we should be dull souls
if we did not feel at least a mild excitement at this conception, this strange blending of physical and spiritual therapy,
as though the healing distillations of Nature were in some
mysterious way caught up and absorbed by the X Force and
carried, on an invisible magnetic tide, into the bodies of the
sick.

All these things, remember, were centred in the not noticeably romantic enviroment of Baker Street. One would
like to know what Sherlock Holmes would have had to say
about them.

And there, for the moment at least, we will pause in our
efforts to give a foolproof definition of what the X Force
really *is,* fully conscious that we may not have satisfied our
imaginary reader who told us that we cannot 'have it both
ways' . . . that we must decide definitely between the
purely psychic and the purely physical. For according to
these distinguished witnesses we can—indeed must—'have
it both ways'. The most we can hope for is that we may at
least have reminded him that it *exists,* that it has presumably always existed, and that its personal application to himself is worthy of more than passing consideration.

Perhaps it was all summed up by one of the greatest
scientists of the present century, Sir Arthur Eddington. Writing in *Space, Time and Gravitation* about the latest revela-
tions of science concerning the nature of the atom, he said:

> And yet in regard to the nature of things, this knowl-
> edge is an empty shell—a form of symbols. It is knowl-
> edge of structural form, not of content. All through the
> physical world runs that *unknown content* which must
> be the stuff of consciousness. Here is a hint of aspects
> deep within the world of physics and yet unattainable
> by the methods of physics.

5. PAUSE WITH A PENDULUM

Perhaps the moment has arrived for another 'progress report'. If we are struggling with material which strains our limited intellectual capacities these brief pauses are a help. There is a long way to go, the road is rocky, tortuous, and often shrouded in mist. A glance over the shoulder may be refreshing.

Summing up the journey to date, we can perhaps reassure ourselves with the thought that we seem to have established the existence of an X Force which has captured the attention and fired the imagination of a number of pioneers throughout.

And with the exception of Dr Ash, in the first chapter, through whose naked hands the Force radiated like a stream of healing light, most of the men whose work we have been considering endeavoured to *harness it to some sort of mechanical device*. Mesmer with his baquet,* Maby with the elaborate instruments through which he channels his natural gift of water-divining, Dr Reich with his orgonoscopes, Eeman with his contraption of copper wires, etc., etc. We might perhaps here find an analogy with the various 'props' employed by mediums in their endeavours to contact the spirits of the departed—the ouija boards, the tambourines, the planchettes, and so on. However, there is one obvious difference between the two forms of apparatus: whereas Mesmer and those who followed him were convinced of the

* Mesmer's baquet was a sort of artificial pool, filled with bottles of 'magnetized' water, connected with silver cords which were held by his patients during treatment. It had all the outward trappings of 'showmanship'—but showmanship, after all, plays its part in therapy.

existence of an X Force *per se*, the spiritualists, in spite of their mediums' 'props', think only in terms of pure spirit, —and as far as I am aware—do not admit the presence of any form of energy except the psychic energy residing in the personalities of those with whom they establish contact from the other side.

Apart from such devices, used by one school or another, there are numerous other instruments which, from time immemorial, have made their appearance in the hands of those who explore these cloudy territories; and of all these the commonest and the most constant is the pendulum. Not a pendulum of any special elaboration, but a simple crystal or metal ball* hanging from a string held between the fingers —on the principle that the mental or spiritual concentration of the holder will dictate the rhythm of its swinging, and that in this rhythm, for those who can interpret it, will be found the answer to certain questions which could not have been solved in any other manner. The pendulum is employed not only by those whose approach might be regarded as 'scientific'—though they are usually inclined to regard it as a somewhat crude method of transmission—but by those who seek for purely spiritual communications. For many of us it has also played its part in the parlour games of our youth.

However, in the hands of the right operator, there is a great deal more to a pendulum than a mere parlour game, as I was to discover on the first occasion when I saw it used, in the house of Dr Aubrey Westlake, to whose researches we are already greatly indebted in the previous chapter.

The story demands a curtain raiser. On the previous night I had been feeling intensely depressed, so much so that I had thought of putting off two friends who were coming to dine— a distant cousin in his late sixties and a young pianist who wanted an opinion on some of his compositions. However, they could not be reached on the telephone, so they came along. I fear that I was bad company. After dinner, the young man played—very well—and I followed him by improvising on some of his themes. This only made things worse, because

* In map-dowsing, as we shall see in a later chapter, the metal from which the ball is manufactured corresponds with the metal which the dowser is seeking on the map—a silver ball to find silver, a copper ball to find copper, and so forth.

—one cannot say this without sounding pompous and conceited—I have a talent for improvising.

When it was over the young man said: 'It is criminal that nothing is done about music such as you have just been playing.'

(All this is apposite to the pendulum episode though it may not appear so.)

I replied by a number of bitter remarks about the music publishing business, and the fame and fortune gained by 'composers' who hadn't a bar of melody in them.

'You must feel pretty hopeless about it sometimes.'

'I do. And not only about music.'

'What else?'

'This book I'm writing. It's beyond me. It's too deep. I shall never finish it.' (This is still strictly apposite.)

My cousin intervened, with a smile. 'I've heard you say that you're hopeless before. But you've always gritted your teeth and gone on to the end.'

'This time I mean it.'

And I did. When they had departed I put through a long-distance call to Dr Westlake, with the intention of cancelling tomorrow's appointment. I would throw the whole thing up—start a novel, write some sketches, practise scales—anything but continue with this back-breaking job. But there was no reply. So I went to bed and took a sleeping pill.

On the following morning I felt a little better. I could at least put on an act and go through with the thing. When I arrived at Dr Westlake's in the afternoon I found that the doctor had been obliged to go out for an hour and I was greeted by his wife—a very charming woman with an engaging smile and nothing at all spooky about her. She was as wholesome as an apple dumpling. She showed me round the premises, which were weirdly beautiful. They lived on the outskirts of a rambling holiday camp, which Westlake had created on lands bequeathed to him by his father. All around us were giant firs in which the wind was playing a long winding melody in five-four time. Music again! I would have liked to write it down. But I must put all that from my mind.

'While we are waiting for the doctor,' said Mrs Westlake, 'is there anything else I can show you?'

'Do you ever take part in his experiments?'

'Sometimes, in a mild sort of way. He seems to think I have some talent with the pendulum.'

'Could I see you using it?'

'Of course.' She looked at me with a twinkle. 'At least it can't do any harm.'

We went back to the house and sat down at a table in the sitting-room.

On the table she laid out three things:

1. A metal foot-rule, such as one sees used by carpenters. It was divided into centimetres. She asked me to put my right thumb on the end of it, explaining—if you can call it an explanation—that the swing of the pendulum would reveal on the scale the boundaries of the field of my personality and my mental condition.

2. A wooden box containing thirty-eight glass phials standing on end. They looked like little sample bottles of scent.

She explained that each of the phials contained the extract of some flower or herb or tree which had therapeutic properties in cases of psychological disturbance.

'Are these the Bach remedies?'

She nodded.

I began to be very interested. Dr Edward Bach was a romantic figure—a Harley Street bacteriologist—who had suddenly thrown up his practice to bury himself in Wales, to hunt for herbs which he felt had greater potencies than were generally acknowledged. In all, he discovered thirty-eight, and to each of these he ascribed very definite functions. Thus:

> Mimulus for Fear
> Star of Bethlehem for Shock
> White Chestnut for Obsessional Thoughts
> Impatiens for Irritability

By an ironic turn of fate Bach's remedies killed him, for with each discovery he suffered in an extreme degree the physical and emotional disorders to which the flower was an antidote.

3. The third object on the table was the pendulum itself—a small cut crystal attached to a slender thread.

'Let's begin,' said Mrs Westlake in the most practical tone. 'I want you to touch each bottle in turn with the thumb of your left hand, keeping your right thumb on the end of this scale. When you touch a bottle that reacts to anything that's wrong the pendulum will swing out at an angle. Ready?'

She took up the pendulum between her thumb and forefinger, and held it a few inches over my hand while I started to touch the bottles. The pendulum was swinging quite regularly up and down, north to south. When I touched the fifth bottle, it swung violently at an angle of about forty-five degrees.

Mrs Westlake lifted this bottle from the box and put it on the table, at the same time making an adjustment on the scale.

I continued to touch the bottles. To most there was no reaction, but by the time we had reached the end of the line four of them had responded and had been removed from the box.

'Let's see what we have here,' said Mrs Westlake, laying the pendulum down beside her. She read out the names on the labels.

'Gorse.'

'That sounds prickly.'

She laughed as though the remark had been really funny.

'Then . . . let's see . . . this is willow. And this is cherry plum. And . . . the label's faded on this one . . . this is oak.'

'And what do all those mean?'

'I haven't a clue. But the doctor will tell you when he comes.'

And the doctor did tell me, when he walked through the door a few minutes later—a lithe, white-bearded figure in his early seventies, radiating health and that strange aura of sheer goodness which I was to encounter so often in my journeyings.

He took up the bottles one by one.

'Gorse.' He raised his eyebrows. 'We use that in cases of . . . hopelessness.'

'Willow.' He closed his eyes for a moment. 'That stands for frustration. For people who feel they are in the wrong job.'

'Cherry plum.' He looked me straight in the eye. 'This is not so admirable. It reacts to people who are inclined to blame others for their own shortcomings.'

He took up the last bottle, and smiled. 'Oak. This is better. It means that in spite of everything you can summon up the strength to carry on.'

He turned to Mrs Westlake. 'And now, my dear, what about a nice cup of tea?'

I have a faint fear that this story may sound as trivial as a recital of any fool's experience with Madame Zaza, the

buxom clairvoyant who is eternally perched on the end of
the pier, wreathed in soiled mauve tulle.

I also have a faint hope that it may not sound quite so
silly as that, providing that you accept its veracity. (For
which, admittedly, there are no witnesses except myself and
the Westlakes.)

Because you must remember that the Westlakes knew
nothing whatever about me . . . the real, inside me. They
knew that I had written a large number of books, with some
degree of success, and that I could be described, without
irony, as 'a well-known author', who was presumably well
satisfied with his status in the world. They had no possible
means of guessing that behind this comfortable façade there
was a hopelessness, a bitter frustration because I was not at
that very moment recording the melody of the pine trees, together with a contemptible and apparently ineradicable tendency to attribute this failure to others. And finally, a grim
determination to go on.

All this was clear to the intuitive genius of Dr Westlake,
in thirty seconds, through the medium of the gorse, the willow, the cherry plum and the oak. I doubt whether Madame
Zaza often scores four bulls, dead centre, in quite so short a
time.

6. THE BLACK BOX

> . . . I don't know, can't be sure
> But there was something in it, tricks and all!
> Really, I want to light up my own mind.
> But what I mean to add is also true.
>
> ROBERT BROWNING: *Mr Sludge, 'The Medium'*

Of all the instruments ever devised to harness the X Force none has ever been as complex as the Black Box, either in its physical construction, or in the theories and practices of those who use it.

What is the Black Box? This is a question easier to ask than to answer. I have spent several years of patient research trying to formulate an answer that would be comprehensible not only to myself but to the general public, and I am still going round in circles. At the conclusion of a sensational trial in the Queen's Bench Division of the British High Court of Justice, which occupied the Court's attention for two long weeks in the summer of 1960, the Box still kept its secrets. The learned judge admitted that he could not make head or tail of it. However, the judge *did* allow that there was a 'great body of opinion' in modern Britain that believed in the Box, a body of opinion that it was 'impossible to ignore'. He also found conclusively in favour of the sincerity and the integrity of the Box's principal modern protagonist, George de la Warr, of the Delawarr Laboratories in the City of Oxford.

But what *is* it? We shall have to face up to this unanswerable question sooner or later, so we had better get it over.

It all began in San Francisco, about fifty years ago, with an American doctor called Albert Abrams. There are two reasons for believing that Abrams was not a charlatan. Firstly, he was extremely rich, and had no temptation to deviate from the path of pure research. Secondly, his medical record was of exceptional brilliance, not only in America but in Europe, where he graduated from Heidelberg with first-class honours as M.A. and M.D., with the gold medal of the University.

The birth of the Box—like the birth of penicillin—was the result of an accident.* One day Abrams was conducting a clinical examination of a patient which involved percussing the abdomen. During this examination his assistant happened to switch on an X-ray apparatus standing a few feet away. Whereupon the percussion note, which had previously been 'resonant', like the sound in the echo chamber of a movie studio, suddenly went flat and dead. This intrigued Abrams so much that he persuaded the patient to take part, there and then, in an experiment, by changing his position in relation to the machine. A few minutes later he had made another startling discovery. The percussion note only went dead *when the patient stood facing east or west; it did not occur when he faced north or south.*

At this precise moment Mesmer must have turned sharply in his grave, for it was Mesmer, a century and a half before, who had first insisted on the 'polarity' of the human body.

To suggest that this was the 'birth of the Box' is a gross over-simplification, but at least it confirmed Abrams in some of the fundamental ideas without which the Box might never have come into existence. One of these was that the basis of disease might be electronic rather than molecular or cellular. To put it in another way, he believed that a diseased condition would not only affect tissues at a cellular level but would also 'entail changes in the electronic constitution of the atoms which were the basic constituents of the molecules composing the body cells. He also believed that such electronic changes would be bound to cause a *variation in the radiations emitted by the affected tissue,* which it would be

* The essential facts about the Abrams story are exhaustively catalogued by J. O. Wilcox in his book *Radionics,* published by Herbert Jenkins. It would have saved me a great many headaches if I had applied to Mr Wilcox for his kind permission to quote his account verbatim. I did not do so for the simple reason that the average reader might have found it largely unintelligible. It was only after many hours spent in having it 'translated' to me by friends with a scientific training that I was able to produce this brief and crude account of it. For those with the necessary scientific background *Radionics* should prove one of the most stimulating books they will ever read.

possible to detect instrumentally if only a sufficiently sensitive instrument could be devised.' *

And the Box which was the eventual outcome of these theories? It began with a metal disc, suspended by an assistant who also held a specimen of diseased tissue, while at the same moment Abrams percussed the patient's stomach. From this point it developed into a fairly simple piece of electrical apparatus provided with a calibrated dial. By adjusting the dial, after much trial and error, he discovered that there were certain definite rates of radiation from every disease which could be fixed and established by numbers on the dial. Thus, supposing that his experiments had taught him to associate the disease of diabetes with the number twelve, and supposing that he suspected the patient of this disease, he would set the dial to twelve, contact the patient's stomach with the disc on his apparatus, and begin the process of percussion. If there was a reaction, he concluded either that the patient was diabetic or that he had a *tendency* towards diabetes, for one of the most remarkable mysteries of the Box—a mystery on which many of its modern exponents insist—was that it appeared to be able to detect the presence of certain diseases before they had actually developed.

But the greatest mystery of all lay in the fact that although Abrams was using a piece of electrical equipment he was not—and he knew that he was not—dealing with an electrical phenomenon as such. There was no such thing as a 'live circuit' in the ordinary electrical sense. To quote Mr Wilcox for the last time: *'The radiations (for want of a better term) which he was by this means able to detect and identify were something quite unknown to classical science.'*

So once again we find ourselves confronted by the X Force. This is another over-simplification, for as we study the later developments of the Box, and the philosophy of its exponents, we shall find that the *thought* of the person using it plays a vital part in the efficacy of its operations. Indeed, we may later come to the conclusion that even the most elaborate Boxes of the present decade are only instruments, of increasing delicacy and complexity, for reinforcing and pin-pointing the power of pure thought. We may suspect that in other hands Abrams's Box might not have proved so competent a diagnostician.

* J. O. Wilcox, *Radionics.*

Before the reader dismisses the foregoing pages as a far-
rago of nonsense let us draw his attention to an historical
fact which may perhaps give pause to even the most orthodox member of the medical profession, if he were previously
unaware of it.

In the early 'twenties Abrams brought his Box to England,
with regrettable results. Instead of being seriously considered
by the medical profession it became a Mayfair talking point.
However, the doctors were at length compelled to acknowledge its existence, if only because so many of their rich and
fashionable patients were demanding to know more about it.
And so, in the summer of 1924, a committee of the British
Medical Association was appointed to investigate its claims,
under the chairmanship of Sir Thomas (later Lord) Horder.
No more respectable board of inquiry could be imagined.
The B.M.A. was, and still is, one of the most staunchly en-
trenched fortresses of orthodoxy in Europe, and Sir Thomas
himself was chief physician to His Majesty King George V.
The Box, it was confidently expected, would be swiftly exposed as the fraud it undoubtedly was, in the opinion of the
great majority of the Harley Street pundits.

Unfortunately for these gentlemen the Box refused to be
dismissed so lightly. It came out of the investigation with
flying colours. I quote from one of the most succinct of many
accounts of this strangely neglected episode:

> The Committee's report was startling. Tests, it said,
> had been arranged under suitable supervision; the results
> had been carefully evaluated; and the Committee had
> come to the conclusion that *no more convincing exposi-
> tion of the reality of the phenomena could reasonably be
> desired*. Not merely was it satisfied that the claims about
> the diagnostic value of the method were proven; two of
> its members, Sir Thomas Horder being one, had ac-
> tually felt an alteration in their abdominal muscles at the
> time when—if the therapeutic claims were to be be-
> lieved—they should have expected to feel them. As they
> could not have been told what to expect, this could not
> have been from suggestion—not, at least, on a conscious
> level.*

Here, one would have thought, was explosive material.
Here was a new theory of medicine, and a new method of

* Brian Inglis, *Fringe Medicine* (Faber & Faber, 1964).

diagnosis, employing 'radiations unknown to classical science', and . . . it worked. It even worked on the eminent stomach of the King's own doctor! Even if they did not understand *how* it worked, surely the committee should have endeavoured to find out? But this would have involved them in an admission of the existence of the X Force, and—as we have observed from Mesmer onwards—this is something that no respectable orthodox body can ever bring itself to do. So nothing was done at all. 'It would be premature', said the committee, 'to hazard any hypothesis.' And therefore it would be 'unethical' for doctors to use it. A conclusion suggesting that the medical interpretation of what is 'unethical' must differ widely from that of the man-in-the-street.

I can add a melancholy little postscript to this story.

Abrams died only a few weeks after the Committee had condemned him—some say of a broken heart. The Box gradually ceased to be a Mayfair talking point, and orthodoxy congratulated itself on the elimination of a tiresome and inexplicable interruption of their well-ordered lives. But there were some of us who could not forget this mystery, and when I later found myself next to Horder at a dinner-party— he had then become Lord Horder—I persuaded him to talk shop, and steered the conversation round to the subject of the Box. At this distance of time I will not presume to recall dialogue, but one sentence echoes clearly over the years. He said: 'I have rather a guilty conscience about it.' Maybe he was remembering that inexplicable twitch in his stomach. He also gave me the impression that he was personally interesting himself in raising funds for a further investigation.

It was too late. Horder was a sick man, and before he could do any more he was dead, stricken by a coronary thrombosis. The one really vital figure in European medicine, the one man who had not only the power to enforce an inquiry but the imagination and the generosity to abide by its findings—which would have brought the X Force on to the front page of the *Lancet*—had vanished from the scene.

But the Box did not die. It proliferated, in England, in France, in America, in many shapes, and sizes, and designs, some of them quite obviously suspect, some of them inexplicable, and many of them madly unpredictable. Among the latter must be mentioned the machines operated by Ruth Drown, who was the Box's chief champion in the United States. In 1950 the American Medical Association's Journal reported on investigations that had been conducted at the request of some of her supporters in the University of Chicago. She was given ten blood specimens to work on; her diagnoses of the first three were so inaccurate that further tests were abandoned.

And yet, in spite of such local set-backs—which must be openly admitted, unless one is intolerably wide-eyed—the Box has not died. It marches on. At the moment of writing, in England alone there are over a thousand Boxes in constant use, 'broadcasting' treatments to 10,000 or more patients simultaneously. I have these figures on the authority of George de la Warr, who produces them, fighting a lone battle from his Oxford citadel.

Some of these Boxes are highly complicated and so are the theories which de la Warr has formulated in the course of using them.

But before examining them I think it is high time that we lightened these pages by telling a story.

7. THE CHART OF THE HIDDEN FISH

The queerest document that came my way during this stage of our journey was the Chart of the Hidden Fish.

Now that I have written those words they recall something that one of Rider Haggard's heroes might have discovered mouldering in a cave of the Andes, scrawled in human blood, marking the site of buried treasure. The surroundings were not so romantic. The chart lay spread out on a desk in the study of a charming little house in the town of Bridport in Dorset. Instead of being written in human blood it had been run off a duplicating machine. It was a map of the British Isles, showing the area of the North Sea, bounded by Ireland to the west, the Faroes to the north, the coast of Norway to the east, and the coast of France to the south.

All the same, it marked buried treasure. The treasure was fish—to be precise, shoals of herring. For the past six weeks, according to the witness of the chart, they had been slowly swimming southwards to warmer waters. On July 7th they had been in the same latitude as the Norwegian coastal town Stavanger. They had travelled down at the rate of about seven miles a day. In the first week of September, which was when I saw them on the map, they had passed the Dogger Bank, swimming rather more swiftly, and were at a point between the 54th and 53rd latitude, about a hundred miles out to sea off the English coast.

All these fish had transmitted their whereabouts by 'radionics'—a word that begins to sound as though it covers a multitude of mysteries—from the dark waters of the North Sea to a little Box.

This sentence announces a miracle which the reader—for a few moments—must be tolerant enough to 'take as read'. When I write that those fish had 'transmitted their whereabouts' I do not mean that they *might* have done so, nor that some eccentric person, after a dainty breakfast of toadstools and hyena's milk, had twiddled a lot of dials and seen shoals of herrings floating across the ceiling. Those fish *had* communicated through the Box as clearly as though each of them had been personally equipped with a broadcasting apparatus.

We are forty years from Abrams. Behind us lie forty years of thoughts—sometimes cloudy, of visions—often blurred—of claims and counter claims—many of them admittedly ridiculous. But the Box, as we have seen, has persisted. And the fact that it can be used in so strange an experiment as the one we have just witnessed suggests that the range of its activities has been greatly extended.

In the course of these forty years a number of techniques have slowly emerged in the use of the Box, so that nowadays those who practise radionics have a large body of experience on which to draw. These techniques often vary according to the individual operator, but one of them has been universally adopted because it seems to be basic to the whole conception. To fix it clearly in the reader's mind I will call it the blood-spot technique.

Here is what happens. If a blood-spot of a patient is placed in the Box—it might be the fin of a fish or even the leaf of a tree but for the sake of simplicity we will, for the moment, confine ourselves to the blood-spot of a human being—and if the *thought* of the patient is held very clearly in the mind of the operator, he can establish a 'rapport' with the patient. And once this 'rapport' is established he can, by a process of elimination, and by further techniques, correctly diagnose the patient's disability and—in some cases—do much to correct it.

Supposing that you were watching an operator working a Box. He puts in a blood-spot—or a piece of human hair, or a spot of rust from a fruit tree. The next thing he does is to set his dials according to the disease rates which were first established by Abrams (see page 55). Since Abrams's time the number of these rates has multiplied exceedingly; nowadays there are several thousands of them corresponding to all the ills to which the flesh—or the mind—is heir.

And now comes the strangest technique of all. Having put on his blood-spot, and set his dials to begin his 'process of elimination', and holding in his mind the thought of the person, animal or plant concerned, he proceeds to stroke a rubber membrane which is set into the Box, with a rapid movement of the fingers of his right hand. When his dials are rightly set—in other words when he is on the right 'wavelength', as it were, for a diseased condition—the rubber membrane suddenly 'resists' and makes a clicking noise. The name given to this phenomenon is the 'stick'.

If I have seen and heard this happen once I have seen it happen fifty times. The rubber does 'stick' and it does make a clicking sound. As it is not connected with anything—no wires, nor screws, nor gadgets of any sort—there can be no question of a mechanical trick. Nor is there the smallest reason to assume any deception, voluntary or involuntary, on the part of the operators. I watched their fingers very carefully, and where the rubber 'stuck' there was no sign of alteration in pressure or pace or rhythm. I also tried, time and again, to make it 'stick' myself. I have a pianist's fingers; they are strong and not insensitive; but the rubber would not 'stick' for me.

I was so fascinated by this particular aspect of the Box that later, in a long correspondence of questions and answers between de la Warr and myself, I asked him to enlarge upon it. His comments were illuminating. After observing that the Box 'merely acts as a means of detecting the thought processes of the operator during diagnosis' he writes:

At the 'Moment of Yes' in the operator's mind . . . ('Yes, Mrs Smith has a mineral deficiency of iodine') . . . there is a physical change in the operator. *His whole body becomes a detector*. Especially, in this instance, his skin.

This is, of course, a mystery, but there are some mysteries which seem to hold a glimmer of light in their dark centre and this is one of them. The light, for a brief instant, glows more brightly, as he continues:

The dial settings of the resonators in the Box *pre-set the vibrations on the Detector in order to assist the energy patterns on the hand of the operator*. And this, needless to say, aids the frictional response.

The light almost flickers out again, but a faint outline remains, as though we had pushed open the door of a dark room and seen, traced on an empty wall, a luminous shadow —the shadow of the X Force.

After which, speaking strictly personally, I feel a strong desire for another story. Let us get back to our fish.

This story, though it is very brief, is so extraordinary that if it is to make its proper impact, if it is to bear the stamp of truth, we should know something of the person who tells it.

Her name is Mrs Sanctuary, and she is the wife of Harry Sanctuary, the man who found the fish mentioned at the beginning of our chapter, and continues to find them. At the moment all we know about the Sanctuarys is that they live in a charming little house in Bridport, and the reader might well suspect that any man who indulged in such bizarre activities must be some sort of wizard or necromancer. This is the very last description that could apply to Mr Sanctuary. To call him a 'successful business-man' would give a false impression of so scholarly a person; but for the purpose of our inquiry it is important to note that he *is* a business-man, a highly respected director of a commercial firm, in his early sixties, with a background that might have come straight out of Trollope—a quiet background of conservative gentlefolk whose sons, when their vocations were being considered, had not much choice between the Church, the Services, and the Law. As it happens, Harry Sanctuary went into the navy, via the Royal Naval Colleges Osborne and Dartmouth which have never, as far as one is aware, given advanced necromancy much prominence in their curriculum.

The little story is coming in a moment, but first there is one other thing to which I must call attention. And this is the 'aura of goodness' which surrounds not only Sanctuary but his wife and indeed his whole household. We have noticed this 'aura' before in our encounters with the men and women of the radiesthetic world. The sceptic may discount it, and obviously, within his limits, the sceptic is right to do so; there have been murderers who have looked like angels and sadists who have gone through the world disguised by a mask of tenderness. I myself have been 'had for a sucker' on quite a number of occasions, by experts in the telling of hard luck stories. But I do not believe that one is exceptionally gullible nor that one's instinct is invariably wrong. And always, in the radiesthetic circle, there has been this feeling that one was in the presence of virtue and truth—even if at times their vision of truth did not quite correspond with one's own. It was as though, in their constant journeyings through the realms of the spirit, some of the radiance which they had discovered had lingered about them.

And now for our story.

'It was in September of 1958', said Mrs Sanctuary, 'that Harry was given one of the most dramatic proofs of the sort of "rapport" that you've already witnessed. We were having a holiday on the West Coast of Ireland, and as usual Harry had spent a large part of his time dowsing in one way or another—sometimes with a pendulum, sometimes with a rod, sometimes with a Box. Obviously, the Box is used for the more serious experiments, which need a lot of time and concentration. But he can't carry a Box about him on a country walk so he puts a pendulum in his pocket. Just in case. Sometimes I think that if we were to go to a race meeting he'd take out his pendulum and start dowsing the race-card.'

Harry shook his head emphatically. He is a man with an agreeable sense of humour but it was evident that the idea did not appeal to him at all. 'I should do no such thing,' he said. 'I have a gift, and I hope I do not abuse it.'

'But I was only joking.'

'Yes, my dear. But you know that I would never do a thing like that.'

(I have recorded this interruption because it throws an interesting side-light on character.)

'Anyway,' continued Mrs Sanctuary, 'the Irish experience really was remarkable. One evening Harry suddenly decided to dowse for herrings on the Box.'

Here it was my turn to interrupt. 'How do you mean . . . dowse for herrings?'

'I had worked out a technique for it,' he said. 'Very briefly it consisted in taking the scales from live fish and returning the fish to the sea. These scales gave me a number rate on the Box. Is that clear?'

It was as clear as it was ever likely to be so I said 'Yes'. And indeed, it *is* possible to imagine some sort of strange radionic communication between a living creature and a portion of the body of one of its fellow creatures.

'So Harry went off to his room with a large scale map and I sat down to read a book. About twenty minutes later he came down in a state of considerable excitement. He had found his herrings, which didn't surprise me because, well, he usually finds what he is looking for. But he had found them in such extraordinary quantities that he could hardly believe the message the Box was sending. He kept on saying, "The sea must be stiff with them."

'And that', she concluded, 'is the end of the story.'

'Not quite, my dear. For as you will remember, on the next day those herrings swam into the respectable columns of the *Irish Times*.'

'I thought it was the *Daily Express*.'

'Possibly. In any case, they were reported in such quantity that the editor thought them worthy of a news story.'

If this story is true, it is a miracle.

If it is not true, the reader must be prepared to make two assumptions, and to stand by them.

The first assumption is that the recorder of the story—myself—is either a liar or a nitwit, either a grossly dishonest reporter or a pathetically gullible creature who believes everything that everybody tells him, going through life dipping his pen—presumably a goose's feather—into any sort of ink that may be to hand, providing that it comes in a pretty bottle.

The reader is entitled to make this assumption; it has been made before. However, he would still have to explain away the newspaper reports.

The second assumption I will not grant so readily. Harry Sanctuary may have his head in the air—which in any case is better than having his head in the gutter, like some who shall be nameless—but his feet are on very solid ground. It is Trollope territory. The Church, the Army and the Law. I don't know his politics but I would guess that he is an old-fashioned Liberal. He is sensitive, widely read, and he and his charming wife lead lives of modest elegance. And always there is that 'aura of goodness'.

I have concentrated on only one aspect of the activities of this remarkable man because the fish story seems important enough to stand on its own, illustrating as it does the almost limitless range of the radiesthetic faculty as it can be applied to modern life. However, like most of his fellows he is many-sided. He believes that there are very few human, animal, or vegetable disorders on which the Box, or the pendulum, or the divining rod, may not have some useful comment to make. Thus, while I was staying with him, he employed the Box to dowse the dahlias in his herbaceous border. It came back with a swift and emphatic diagnosis of leaf rust! And within the limits of his time as a hard-worked business-man he uses it to treat those among his friends who are sick. I cannot report on any of these cases because I did not investigate them, but I believe him when he tells me that the results of this Box therapy have been in *some* cases spectacular. He stressed the 'some'. Radiesthetists are seldom braggarts. When you are in touch with the infinite you do not claim to be infallible.

While I remember it I think I should also note a certain psychological 'attunement' between Harry and others who are concerning themselves with these mysteries. Like Professor Maby he is acutely—some might even say morbidly—affected by thunderstorms. And like almost every other advanced dowser that I have met he has occasional 'black-outs'. This does not mean that he swoons or loses consciousness—he is not at all the willowy type—but rather that something in him seems to dry up, as though Nature had said to him, 'Thus far, and for the moment, no further.'

One remark of his especially underlined this 'attunement'. He said:

'The curse of all dowsing is interference.'

These were precisely the same words that Professor Maby had used, when he had been speaking of emotional onlookers who 'bumped the ether'. They were the same words—*mutatis mutandis*—that an old shepherd in Wiltshire had used when he had thrown his dowsing twig on to the turf and looked up to curse the giant electric pylons that were striding across the downs. And the same words used by a delicate lady in a floppy hat on the lawn of a stately home, when she had glanced over her shoulder at a black thundercloud hurrying towards us from the neighbouring hills. She pushed her elegant little divining rod back into her crocodile bag. 'Such a bore,' she pouted. 'Nature will always *interfere*.'

And that reminds me that as yet, in this rambling chapter, I haven't mentioned what was for me the most important point of all.

For it was in Harry Sanctuary's garden that I first discovered that I was myself a water-diviner.

The gift of dowsing, according to Harry, is not much to boast about. He claims that the number of people who have it greatly exceeds the number of those who do not*, though their success in using it naturally depends on the spirit of their approach and their willingness to conform to a certain standard of technique.

All the same it is a rather thrilling experience when you first feel the rod surging in your hands. We walked out on to a lawn not quite so large as a tennis-court under which, apparently, there were several sizeable streams. At first we used the rod together, with my fingers gripping the right prong of the fork and Harry's gripping the left. We paced forward slowly and suddenly, without any warning, the rod leapt upwards, as though an invisible hand had wrenched it. I was surprised by the force of the movement.

But the real thrill was to come when I tried on my own. However much you may trust a man, however convinced you may be of his integrity, you cannot quite forget, when you are merely sharing an experience of this nature, that at the other end of the rod there is a human agent, who might be the victim of auto-suggestion, or subject to some sort of nervous reaction which was dictated by memory or wishful thinking, rather than by the immediate dictation of hidden forces.

Whereas, on this occasion, I was very determined to clear my mind of any form of auto-suggestion. It would not be true to say that I intended to 'fight' the rod; that would have got nobody anywhere. But I certainly was not going to help it. My attitude to the rod was similar to that of a theatrical producer sitting back in the stalls during an audition of bit-part players. 'Come on . . . show me what you can do.'

The rod showed me, beyond any shadow of doubt.

'Walk steadily,' said Harry. 'At about the pace of a slow march. Grip the ends very firmly indeed. Hold it in a strictly horizontal position. Whatever you do, don't change the position of your hands. Don't alter the tension. Keep them as steady as a rock. O.K.? Carry on.'

I started to walk. If it were possible to 'set one's mind in a grim line', like the mouths of rugged heroes in romantic novels, my mind would certainly have been set in that way. I felt nothing, I did not expect to feel anything, and my fists

---

* Professor Maby, as we have seen, would not rate the proportion so highly. And he is insistent that even the comparatively few 'natural' dowsers must be prepared to submit themselves to a rigorous training before their findings can be trusted with any degree of certainty.

were clenched so tightly that if there were any manifestation at all it would have to be something pretty big.

And it was. Whish! Up went the rod at about the fiftieth step, and stayed there pointing to the sky. Again there was the sense that an invisible hand had wrenched it, but this time the strength of the force was greatly increased. It would be easy to over-stress the dramatic nature of this moment . . . but for me it had drama. It was a high spot, a culmination point in the story over which I had so long been puzzling. As though one had been painfully building up the personality of a leading character in a novel, trying to make him come to life. And as though one had suddenly turned a corner and met him face to face.

8. MAGIC OR MOONSHINE?

I consider the Delawarr Laboratories to be the most singular
place in the world. Here one can feel the pulse-beat of that
mysterious life which death cannot interrupt. I consider its
work of far greater importance than the grand spectacle of
the Russian and American satellites. For our body is a universe teemig with galaxies of worlds of its own, and a study
of this is of much more import than journeys to the moon.

JEAN COCTEAU

Authors who write books of this nature should perhaps tell
their readers when to skip.

If you have had enough of the Box* you had better turn
to page 88. There, admittedly, we shall be sailing into
deeper waters, but it will be plainer sailing for the very reason that we shall be so far from land. As long as we stay
with the Box, navigation is apt to be tricky, because we are
still, as it were, within sight of the shores of the material
world, still threading our way through a great many extremely substantial rocks. We cannot just look up to the sky
and set a course by the stars. Would that we could! We have
to go on twisting our dials, referring to our books of rates
and numbers, stroking our rubber membranes, collecting our
blood-spots, etc., etc.

Is it all worth-while? Would it not be simpler merely to
think? Simplest of all . . . to pray? Do we really need all
these gadgets? In a previous chapter we suggested that, quite
possibly, we didn't. We ventured the opinion that we might
find in the end that the Box was merely a device for 'pin-
pointing the power of pure thought'.

But even if this *is* its only function, surely it is one which
would still deserve our consideration?

Look at it like this. Here, in the seventh decade of the

* In order that this section may not stretch to an intolerable
length the final technical 'break-down' of the Box—in other words
what we find when we open it—is relegated to the appendix.
Although it is extremely complicated there may be some who
will feel it worthy of study. However, the present chapter can, I
hope, be understood without this extra effort.

twentieth century, in broad daylight, in a respectable suburb of the city of Oxford, is a man by name George de la Warr who claims to have done something which might be described as harnessing the lightning of the mind—the universal mind. The metaphor is open to objection, for unless one is a Shelley, endowed with the genius to build a dome of many-coloured glass with a stroke of the pen, one is unlikely to find a single phrase to encompass so many marvels.

But *are* they marvels? Is the Box, at best, an illusion, at worst a conjuring trick? You will find plenty of people to tell you that it is the latter. Maybe it will help us to make up our minds if we refer to the Court case of 1960 in which the Box, via the person of de la Warr himself, was subject to a pitiless scrutiny.

The Philips *v.* de la Warr case was heard before Mr Justice Davies in the Queen's Bench Division of the High Court of Justice between June 20th and July 6th, 1960. The plaintiff was a certain Miss Philips and her sister Mrs Holdsworth; the action was for fraud; and the damages demanded amounted to £185.

In 1956 Miss Philips bought a diagnostic instrument, a book of rates and a set of detail cards, and began a course of lessons. It was alleged that she practised for several months without making progress, and that she was reduced from a cheerful, hopeful person to a frustrated and tearful nervous wreck. She therefore suffered inconvenience, injury to health, and loss of earnings. She claimed that in selling her the diagnostic instrument Mr de la Warr fraudulently represented that distinctive waves, vibrations or radiations were associated with all forms of matter, and that these could be identified by means of the instrument, which, with the aid of a bloodspot, could be used for the diagnosis and treatment of diseased conditions of the mind and body. More generally, she also alleged that Mr de la Warr was an exponent and practitioner of the pseudo-science of radionics. The Judge, addressing Miss Philips's counsel, Mr Karmel, expressed the matter very simply: 'Is [it] your case that the whole thing is nonsense?' Mr Karmel replied that it was; Mr de la Warr could not have had an honest belief that Miss Philips could operate the box. The case therefore turned on whether radionics was nonsense, and whether Mr de la Warr was honestly convinced of the truth of his claims.*

This was the groundwork of the case and for two weeks the prosecution devoted itself to the enjoyable task of tying the de la Warrs into knots. What could be simpler? Could any counsel wish for a more heaven-sent opportunity to exercise his sarcasm, his bluff, down-to-earth, man-of-the-world approach to these matters?

'A mass of mumbo-jumbo . . . a jumble of rubbish,' roared the prosecution.

'The whole "set-up"? A sham. And so were the "numbers" . . . the rate-book.'

'Mr de la Warr himself? A high-pressure salesman. Why, in his evidence he had claimed that he could *actually cure the public through radio and television!*'

(At this point the prosecution was guilty of a misquotation, no doubt unintentional. The word used by de la Warr was not 'cure' but 'treat'.)

In a final sweeping gesture of contempt for the whole body of men and women all over the world who are so painfully grappling with these problems, the prosecutor described them as 'hoodwinked and hoaxed' by practitioners who were 'brazen and composed', led by a man who had an 'utter recklessness for the truth.'

And the result? After a summing-up of three hours, in a tense and crowded court-room, his lordship gave judgment for the de la Warrs. He did not pretend to understand their work, nor to grasp what they meant when they said that all diagnosis and treatment took place 'on a pre-physical plane'. Though he was anxious not 'to express this unkindly' they had made some exaggerated claims, which he called 'shooting a line'. However, this was not necessarily inconsistent with a genuine belief. People often made extravagant claims for things they believed in.

The judge added that there was clearly a great body of opinion favouring a belief in radionics and one which, he expressly stated, it was 'utterly impossible to ignore'. He refused to discount the evidence of radionic practitioners on the grounds that they were connected with Mr de la Warr and were making a good living. He found them no less im-

* The Philips *v.* de la Warr Case (Radionic Association Ltd, Swinbrook, Burford, Oxfordshire).

pressive than the other witnesses. And it was remarkable, in his view, that the prosecution had been unable to call a single witness to support Miss Philips's allegation of fraud. On all points concerning the sincerity of the de la Warrs's belief his findings were decisive.

And after that?

His lordship ordered costs against Miss Philips but—owing to the intolerable injustice of the present state of the law—when the expenses of the losing party are paid by legal aid, the winning party is obliged to pay his own expenses, in spite of a Judge's ruling that he is entitled to costs. As a result, Mr de la Warr suffered a crippling financial blow, in spite of having won a legal and a moral victory.

The financial blow was indeed 'crippling'; the de la Warrs were brought to the verge of bankruptcy; the laboratories were mortgaged to the hilt—and I believe still are; and the work on a number of instruments of fantastic delicacy and complexity was indefinitely delayed.

The critical reader may protest that none of this has any bearing on the actual merits of the Box. I would not entirely agree. For surely, the very fact of de la Warr's integrity is a reason, even if only a negative one, for persevering in our endeavours to understand his theories. And in the courts of British law his integrity has been established beyond the shadow of a doubt.

Another story. A story that may throw a little more light on a phrase that we have used before, when we suggested that the Box might be a device for 'pin-pointing the power of pure thought'.

The scene is the Delawarr Laboratories on the outskirts of Oxford. These consist of a cluster of buildings grouped round a pleasant garden on a little hill from which we can see, in the distance, the dreaming spires of the colleges. The site is symbolic; the University is so near and yet so far. Not for the first time in her history Oxford holds herself coldly aloof from the work of a pioneer. From time to time a professor pays a fleeting visit and there have been occasions when de la Warr has been invited to address select gatherings of scientists connected with the University. Some individual members of his audience have been so startled by what they heard that they made further inquiries, almost against their will; but as yet none has had the energy—or perhaps the courage—to act as a spokesman, let alone a champion. As far as the great body of University opinion is concerned, the laboratories might be a centre of witchcraft.

And indeed, when you first enter them, you might feel that you had strayed into a temple of modern necromancy. The models of 'energy patterns' alone are enough to make the visitor rub his eyes.* One in particular I remember—a three-dimensional model of the ether patterns round a cactus plant. These were detected by the Box during an investigation of the 'space in the immediate vicinity of living things—an investigation which revealed the existence of some extremely complex force fields'. Whatever we may make of that explanation, the model itself is of vibrant beauty; it streams and flows like a piece of music. To a person as scientifically uninstructed as myself it suggested that even if the Box had no other function it might be used to create some very lovely designs—though perhaps the word 'create' is here inapposite. For all the Box was doing in this instance, if we are to believe those who were manipulating it, was to draw from the ether the patterns which were already there, to give them shape and substance. An idea, surely, that might speed a poet's pen, implying as it does that every flower of the field creates, in the air around it, a dancing vibrationary portrait of itself, if only we had eyes to see, a musical echo of its true nature, if only we had ears to hear.

But we were supposed to be telling a story. So let us enter the main laboratory, with Mr and Mrs de la Warr, and take a seat in front of the latest of the Boxes, which is known as a 'Multi-Oscillator Unit and Detector'. It looks like the sort of thing one finds in the control room of an ultra-modern television studio, four feet long, bristling with dials, exquisitely fashioned at great expense.

This machine, by various devices which I do not pretend to understand, is connected with other machines, whose purpose is—to me—equally obscure. But one of them any child could understand, for it looks like just another television set. The only difference is that whereas the screen of an ordinary television set is usually reflecting patterns of peculiar ugliness,

---

* Photographs of such patterns will be found in *A Study of the Ether* by George de la Warr, obtainable from the Delawarr Laboratories, Raleigh Park Road, Oxford. A considerable body of literature on the whole subject is available to any reader who is brave enough to tackle it.

such as the swollen and contorted lips of a pop singer, opening and shutting like a ferocious sea anemone, this particular screen is reflecting patterns of the utmost delicacy and grace, golden threads that twine and twist in a sort of abstract ballet, as though they are responding to the direction of an unseen 'etheric' choreographer.

G. K. Chesterton once wrote a story called 'The Wrong Shape' in which he developed the theory that there were certain material objects which, by their very design, proclaimed their inherent evil, as though in the cruel curve of an oriental dagger we might detect the perverted instincts of the man who fashioned it. He might well have turned the theory upside down and called his story 'The Right Shape', on the principle that there are also objects whose outlines declare their intrinsic innocence. Of such a nature, so it seemed to me, was the pattern of the golden threads dancing across that screen.

When we paused for these reflections we were sitting in front of the main Box, about to take part in an experiment. The de la Warrs asked me to 'feed it a thought', and to see what the machine made of it, through the customary process of elimination, employing the classic techniques of stroking the rubber membrane, consulting the Book of Rates,* and adjusting the dials. They also suggested that I should make the thought as improbable and as difficult as possible.

After a few moments' consideration I decided to centre the thought round my very special and important cat 'Oscar'. He happened to be ill at the time and was seldom out of my mind. However, the conception of a sick cat might perhaps be too simple; if the machine 'got' it one would still not be entirely convinced that this was not merely a case of common or garden telepathy, if such a miracle can ever be so described. I therefore decided that the thought should be 'the quintessence of felinity', holding it so firmly in my mind that I felt that I might myself begin to purr if the experiment went on too long.

The experiment did, in fact, go on for over a quarter of an hour, during which time there was a great deal of twisting of dials, writing down of numbers and combinations of numbers, while the operator passed his fingers rapidly over the rubber membrane to select the moment of 'rapport' between his own thought and the appropriate electronic fre-

* See Appendix.

quencies—in other words 'analysing the thought into its con-
stituent frequencies'.*

To cut a long story short, the machine went from the human to the animal, from the animal to the feline, and from
the feline to the abstract, after which things got a bit muddled. But that was good enough for me.

In writing that the *machine* did it I am not forgetting the
fact that the machine did it in harmony—or rapport or 'resonance', or whatever you choose to call it—with the operator. However, we must underline the part played by the machine itself, because I am convinced that if this was not a
case of simple telepathy, at least it was 'telepathy plus', the
'plus' being represented, among other things, by the Book
of Rates. All this, of course, is a very elaborate process which,
if we were uncharitably disposed, would be as suspect as the
most obviously contrived devices of a fashionable séance.
However, I cannot bring myself to believe that two highly intelligent people—people, moreover, who have about them that
'aura of goodness' which I have previously noted in so many
researchers in these fields—could have decided to waste
their lives in indulging in a lot of mumbo-jumbo which has
led them perilously near to the Bankruptcy Courts.

Postscript. Here I take a liberty which may seem unpardon-
able to all those who respect the literary proprieties. I pro-
pose to expose the proofs of this book to the public eye, with
all their scratches, blots, and erasions. Quote, from a bewildered proof-reader:

'Chapter Eight somewhat confuses me. What is not at all
clear—in the account of the screen and the "cat-thought"—
is just what *was* appearing on the screen. If it were lines
and abstract patterns (rather like a TV set that has not been
properly tuned in) how could you or the operator *know* that
it was "cat"? I assume that it was not a cat image that appeared on the screen. Then how did "abstract" make itself
apparent? And "quintessence"? How could you *know?* What,
in fact, was the actual image in relation to your thought?'

1. My own thought—'the quintessence of felinity'—was not
shaped in the image of any particular cat. True, it began with
Oscar, and at the risk of sounding ridiculous it was a thought
that was charged with deep distress. But I deliberately said
goodbye, as it were, to Oscar . . . in his actual shape and
colour; I sent him off the stage, and evoked the cats of all

* See Appendix.

the world. God knows, this is difficult to explain! What I mean is that I tried to feel akin, related to, vibrating with . . . the alley cats of Tangier, the starving kittens of Calcutta, the desolate little strays in the Greenwich Village Humane League on Eighth Avenue in New York City. They were all, now that I am recalling this so vividly, *sad* cats . . . just as my Oscar was a sad cat. Which leads us to the second question.

2. 'It was not a cat image that appeared on the screen.' No. Not an image in the sense of four legs and whiskers and a tail. But it was an image of grace and swift curling lines. No. Prowling lines. Yes. That seems to be the word. Prowling. They flickered and stalked and *prowled*. But there was an overall sadness. Now and then they jerked, as if the muscles were failing. In case this sounds like 'wishful after-thinking'— and I would not rule this out altogether—I might agree to strike out the word 'prowling'. But I could not strike out the 'grace' nor the 'sadness'. The lines were, in short, tracing the sort of pattern which an abstract painter might have traced, given such a theme.

3. 'How did the operator *know* that it was a cat?' By a process of elimination, i.e. by using the Book of Rates. This highly abstruse technique is described in the Appendix as clearly as I could manage, so I will not elaborate it here, beyond saying that the book contains over 7,000 numbers corresponding with every imaginable disease, physical or mental. Just as the Box appears to track down the precise part of the body which is disordered, so, presumably, when the operator is nearing his target he receives signals which switch him over from the human to the animal, and from the animal to the feline.

One last word. In case this 'animal interlude' sounds altogether too fanciful, I can call witnesses of the highest integrity who would be prepared to swear to even stranger examples of de la Warr's 'rapport' with animals. Thus: William Henderson, a gentleman farmer in the county of Somerset, whom I first met in India when he was A.D.C. to the Viceroy. Mr. Henderson has no axe to grind; he is endowed with more than ample means; and he has a lively intelligence which—when he has any spare time—he expresses in painting pictures which are beginning to command respectable prices in the markets of London and Paris.

Well . . . Mr Henderson had a cow, and the cow went sick, and nobody could find out what was the matter with it, and everybody was very worried, because the cow was a very special sort of cow, and worth a great deal of money. And then, somebody said 'send a blood-spot to de la Warr', which sounded to Mr Henderson a most bizarre procedure. However, he sent the blood-spot, and in a few days he received a photograph, taken with the de la Warr camera (an instrument which I have not described in these pages, partly because it is almost inexplicable but principally because de la Warr, through lack of financial backing, is no longer using it). To describe it as a 'Black Box with a camera attached' would be the over-simplification of all time, but at least it will enable us to form a rough mental image of it. The photograph—which was 'generated' solely by the blood-spot—showed a sort of X-ray of the cow's stomach, and in the centre of the stomach a long, black, twisted line. With the photograph came a letter from de la Warr—whom he had never met—suggesting that the cow had swallowed a piece of wire and recommending an immediate operation. Strongly against the advice of most of Mr Henderson's friends the operation was performed, and there was the wire and the cow lived happily ever after.

'Believe it or not.' One has to say this again and again in reporting this sort of story. You are quite entitled to disbelieve it, but you can only do so on the assumption that some of the gentlemen farmers of England must be very odd and spooky individuals, with a strangely perverted sense of humour. And that has not been my personal experience of them.

9. DIALOGUE WITH AN ENIGMA

There are seas to be explored and I can only sail a little way
out and come back with a report that the sea stretches infinitely vast beyond them.

EDMUND GURNEY in the Willet Scripts

In the last three chapters there has been precious little dialogue and all too many enigmas. We will now try to repair
this omission, by a dialogue with de la Warr himself. And
then we can say goodbye to the Box and set our sails for
those deeper waters that lie ahead.

This dialogue is compiled from the answers to a series of
questionnaires which I sent to him over a period of about
six months. There were many questions, some of them so
elementary that he must have needed all his patience to
consider them. There was an even greater number of answers,
some of them of fiendish complexity. If we might allow ourselves a momentary smile—I do not see why, in our ponder-
ings on the nature of the universe, we should rule out the
possibility that Infinity and Universal Mind may have 'enter-
tainment value'—I might mention that whenever a bulky reg-
istered envelope was delivered, bearing the Oxford postmark,
my factotum, Mr Gaskin, was filled with forebodings. It was
going to be a difficult day. Mr Nichols would be late for his
lunch. And when eventually he was persuaded to eat it, he
would almost certainly complain that it was over-cooked.

Having allowed ourselves this brief twitch of the lips I
should like to quote from de la Warr's final letter, at the end
of the correspondence, in which he gives his views as to the
state of mind from which those problems should be approached.

If you could draw a simple analogy between three con-
secutive states of consciousness you could prove that

. MIND is the all important factor in life. We tend to look at everything through the wrong end of the telescope. Assume for the sake of the Theorem of the Three States of Consciousness that there are three progressive states of All-water, Bel-air and No-air. The little fish in the ocean of All-water grows in intelligence but in the limited confines of the fish world. The fish cannot under stand the things that are in the world of Bel-air.

We, who live in Bel-air, cannot understand our next state of No-air where we have no physical body and the Mind is paramount. In the state of No-air we find that our thoughts and our emotions are so very powerful that we have to learn to control them. The Law of the Universe that 'everything shall live in complete harmoney— or else'—clearly operates so powerfully that there are many new things to learn. As all energy is supplied by an *All Pervading Sound* you have to learn to tune in to it to obtain sustenance for your mind.

Now the *common denominator* in All-water, Bel-air and No-air is simply *Mind* and in that order of progression. It is an increasing order. When the fish dies it is of little account, when we die it is of slightly more account, but only because of the degree of mind.

An 'All Pervading Sound'? I am not sure what this means, but it has a curious echo of truth, like some of the lines in Blake's poems, which make no sense at all when you try to pin them down in a normal sequence of subjects, verbs and objects, and yet have a sort of crazy sanity of their own.

Now for my first question:

It seems to me that you have never clearly demonstrated the *therapeutic* powers of the Box. Can this be done? I know that there are thousands of people all over the world at this moment, who are 'on' it, and I know that your files at Oxford afford ample evidence that they have benefited from their treatment, but you have never explained the process in terms that are comprehensible to the average man.

So what would you draw, if you were a cartoonist with a pen in your hand, working to a dead-line, knowing that you had to get over your message to five million stodgy people on a Sunday morning? If I were to put that question to Mr Smith he would probably reply as follows: 'I should draw a lot of wavy lines, in a distinctive pattern, emanating from the patient. The pattern would be something like this:

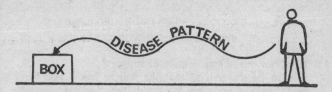

'These lines'—so says Mr Smith—'would represent Disease.'

And then Mr Smith would continue: 'After which I would draw another succession of lines of a contrary nature also emanating from the Box, which would "reverse the Disease pattern".'

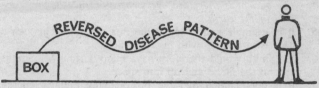

Is this utter balderdash? Or does it contain some grain of truth?

Here is his reply:

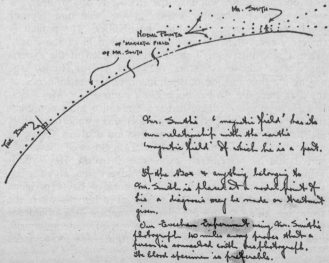

Mr. Smith's 'magnetic field' has its own relationship with the earth's 'magnetic field' of which he is a part.

If the Box or anything belonging to Mr. Smith is placed at a nodal point of his a diagnosis may be made or treatment given.

Our Evesham Experiment using Mr. Smith's photograph 40 miles away proves that a person is connected with his photograph. The blood specimen is preferable.

CAN THE BROADCAST TREATMENT PHENOMENON BE SHOWN DIAGRAMMATICALLY?

1. How can one sketch a state of rapport?
2. It must be understood that the patient has a vast force field that does not obey the usual laws of electro-magnetism (as expounded by Maxwell).
3. As a denizen of earth there is a position in the earth's force field for each person's force field. Not *one* position but an extremely high number of positions even around the circumference of the earth (which is of course a magnet).
4. *The patient is therefore everywhere at once in the force field of the earth.*
5. It is a simple matter to set the Box resonating in such a way as to link up with his force field.
6. Mr Smith would therefore have many virtual Mr Smiths around the globe and up into space.
7. It is not claimed that the Box actually radiates energy in the accepted scientific sense, but it is suggested that it 'toothes in' with the PATIENT-CUM-EARTH relationship.

If our Mr Smith will take the trouble to study these answers again—particularly answer 4—he will find himself pondering a concept of limitless possibilities. 'The patient is therefore everywhere at once in the force field of the earth.' When I read this I was immediately reminded of the experiences of certain investigators, of whom Aldous Huxley was among the first and the most eminent, under the influence of the drug mescalin. In her book *The Infinite Hive** Mrs Rosalind Heywood, a distinguished scholar and a most conscientious reporter, describes her own experiences under this drug, and had she read de la Warr's explanation while in a state of artificially induced clairvoyance she might well have observed that he was merely expressing a truism. Her experiment was carried out under medical supervision with the assistance of a tape-recorder, and the core of her experience was a 'sense of oneness'. The doctor asked her if—when she found one thing taking the place of another—she could see the connection between the two. She replied contemptuously, 'It's quite simple. They are the same thing. It's seeing from

* Chatto & Windus, 1964.

the *middle,* you see. Such words as here or there, far or near, up or down, then or now, were simply not applicable in a world where everything seemed to be in a sphere—a non-spatial one—and where objects were not only perceived from the outside but their "becomingness was also entered into and shared".'

To the plain question: 'How many people has the Box cured?' de la Warr returned no direct answer. He observed: 'This is not a good question. If one were to ask a general medical practitioner this question he could not answer it. Rather inquire what proportion of successful treatments are given. In our case it is about eighty per cent. This is very high because such a large porportion of our patients are "cast-offs" who have been given up by everybody else.'

He added that 'animals are our best patients—a fact that disposes of the explanation put forward of "faith" healing.'

This seems as near as we are ever likely to get to a down-to-earth account of the Box's 'behaviour' and the effects it has on those who are in contact with it. Maybe no such account can ever be written. The fact remains, as we have previously observed, that thousands of people *are* being treated by it, and are prepared to testify in its favour.

The rest of our questionnaire will, I hope, make easier reading.

Question:

From a novelist's point of view I am intensely interested in the STORING of animal magnetism (or the X Force, or whatever we call it). PractICALLY the storing over a long period of time. This is of course basic to the whole conception. (I am right, am I not, in assuming that a blood-spot might be described as a 'repository of resonance'? And am I also right in saying that we might compare this blood-spot with a sort of tiny 'concert hall' in which the music lingered on?)

But to explain this to a wide public one needs very vivid illustrations. Can you supply them?

In his reply de la Warr gives me a gentle rap on the knuckles, beginning by reminding me that 'this storing of energy in inanimate objects such as Atua tends to have overtones of mysticism.'

From there he continues:

I do not understand why the storing of energy is 'basic to the whole conception'. The formless energy pervading the nonmaterial universe and available for all of us to use, is the actual source. Call it Universal Mind. It would appear that the materialization of this energy into space and time seems to need some medium at a particular point in space to aid the process, the actual person making the evocation, etc. I think the patient's blood specimen is merely the focal point of one end of the rapport dual hook-up.

Again, no comment. The meaning is clear enough and is in accord with much that has gone before.

My next question was frankly sensational.

Question:
What is the answer to this rather frightening question:
If a skilled operator, through the Box, can act as the transmitter of curative radiations, could he not also send out malignant radiations? Put another way, if the Box plus the operator can produce harmony, could it not also produce discord? Would it not be a sensationally effective test, for example, if experiments were made on plants with the *deliberate* intention of stunting their growth by maladjustment of the dials? Or is this merely fantasy?

The answer to this is revealing, not only in the theory that it propounds but in the light that it sheds on the mentality of the man himself. De la Warr has a quality that might be described as a sort of compulsive chastity; he is one of the few men I have ever met whom it would be difficult to imagine making a dirty joke.

Here is his brief, heated answer, untouched, even to the split infinitive. (Incidentally, 'Split Infinitive' might not be such a bad title for this book.)

Answer:
To deliberately seek to do harm, *whatever* the means employed, is to make oneself a Black Magician and to fall into alignment with the forces of positive evil.

Experiments on inhibiting growth should be carried out with the greatest circumspection. The Reverend Franklin Loehr has over-stepped the mark by actually cursing a plant for five weeks until it died. We have not experimented with these negative aspects.

This was not enough for me. The Reverend Franklin whom we shall be meeting later, sounded a most engaging person. If I had not been afraid of being misconstrued I should have asked de la Warr for an introduction, and set the reverend gentlemen to work in the garden, cursing the ground elder. As it was I replied:

Question:

Evil. I do not think that you really answered my question. Surely you must see the idea behind it? Every positive demands a negative, and if our Mr Smith is to visualize the Box as a force for good, he must also be able to visualize it as a force for evil. In the last chapter I suggested that you 'shrank away' from this problem. Is it possible that you might now face up to it?

After posting this letter I had misgivings. His reply allayed my anxiety.

Answer:

EVIL AND THE BOX

1. This is something we cannot answer from experience.
2. Logically speaking it would appear that the answer is Yes. But not more so than the general conception of promoting negative thoughts as an individual.
3. The successful use of the Death Prayer is probably rare, in fact I would go so far as to say that the ability to perform this rite is very rare indeed and that its success would be in no way enhanced by a Box.
4. The number of Effigy Dolls sold in Manhattan representing the figure of the Commissioner of Markets, Mr Albert Pacette, for the purpose of sticking pins in them to eliminate him, answers this question. The 'hated' Commissioner is a hale and hearty man (up to the moment of writing).
5. In any case you cannot tune the Box in for a disease and transmit it to a person.

The questionnaire was certainly evoking some unexpected personalities, even though it was serving no other purpose! I should have liked to make further inquiries about Effigy Dolls, for these sinister objects have a long history. And there can be few of us, at some time or other, who have not toyed with the idea of fashioning one for our own malicious uses.

Our task would have been a great deal easier if all his an-swers had been so simple. However, the very nature of some of the questions made this impossible. For example, I felt obliged to attempt, however clumsily, to come to grips with the problem of magnetism, which is inextricably woven into the theory and practice of radiesthesia.

Before referring to this question let us have a little story. Not long ago, in the comfortable dining-room of the Queen's Restaurant, Sloane Square, I was lunching with a lady to whom we referred on a previous page, Mrs Rosalind Hey-wood. It was a stimulating occasion—for me, at any rate. Mrs Heywood has an agreeably astringent intelligence and her critical approach to the problems we were discussing was a wholesome corrective to any tendency to 'take things as read'. Suddenly, while we were waiting for the wine-list, Mrs Heywood paused in the middle of a very caustic commen-tary on some of the more extravagant claims of what may be called 'fringe medicine', and began to fumble in her bag. As she did so she said: 'Whenever I feel that I am being hyper-critical or making too many demands for positive "proof" of this, that or the other, I open my bag and I take out . . . these.' Whereupon, she laid three square metal tubes on the tablecloth. They were magnets.

For the next ten minutes we neglected our luncheon, fas-cinated by the mystery of those magnets. Why did one of them slide across the tablecloth to join the other, when it was placed in a certain position? And why, when it was turned over, did it slide away? What were these strange sym-bols doing? I did not know. Nor did she. Indeed, she ended this little demonstration by what might be called a leading question. She asked: 'What is a magnetic field? It is simply a metaphysical conception.'

If we accept this definition it is possible that my own ques-tions may not seem so crude, nor de la Warr's answers to them so needlessly obscure. The first question was simply:

Question:
What is a magnetic field?

Answer:
1. Language will not satisfactorily answer this. Ferro-magnetism is still a largely unexplained phenomenon.
2. The work we have described in 'The Network of The Ether' postulates and demonstrates the existence of a

force field *around all things*, including magnets. These force fields are all related and a correct relationship aids the establishment of rapport.

3. Critical rotational positioning is one way to seek rapport.

The phrase 'critical rotational positioning' takes us back nearly fifty years to Dr Abrams's consulting room, when he first discovered that rapport—though he would have called it 'resonance'—was affected by the position in which the patient was standing in relation to the magnetic poles. The bewildered reader may take some small comfort from the thought that however obscure the practitioners of radiesthesia may be, there is a remarkable consistency in their obscurity.

Question:
Is the magnetic field of the earth related to the magnetic field in the Box?

Answer:
1. Yes. The tiny magnet in the Box can obviously be adjusted in relationship to the earth's magnetic field.
2. The blood specimen of the patient can be placed in the correct position in the Box in relationship to the *tiny* magnet.
3. Thus a state of rapport with Mr Smith can be sought by correct positioning of blood specimen and the tiny magnet.

And there we will leave this matter, if only because we are never likely to come to a clear understanding of it, however many questions we may ask about it.

Two last questions and we shall have done. These concerned music and colour, relating the two to the whole radiesthetic conception. We have made use of the musical analogy earlier in the chapter. Could colour have a similar application? I was the more interested to know his views on this because one of the most fascinating instruments that I had seen at the laboratories was called the colourscope, in which colour was used in the treatment of certain diseases. Wild horses would not drag me into a discussion of *that*, at this juncture; we should all end up by rolling in the straw with foam spouting from our mouths. But I felt it necessary to ask the questions because I feel music and colour had always been the two animating impulses of my own life; and always, even as a child, I had a curious sense that they overlapped, that there was dark music and light music, and that there were colours that sang in different keys.

Music—colour—therapy—the   box . . . what   comment had this extraordinary man to make?

Question:

Music

'All art tends to the condition of music' (Walter Pater). I believe this to be profoundly true in aesthetics. Has it a wider application, for instance to your own work? Comments? When we were talking about Mesmer last week I mentioned the theory that animal magnetism can be 'stored'. Can music also be 'stored'? For instance, is it conceivable that an original manuscript of Chopin might produce some sort of musical pattern or reaction? (I am looking ahead 1,000 years.) But the whole idea is rich in poetry.

Colour

How far is the role of colour basic to your conceptions? I rather got the impression during my visit to Oxford that colour was in the nature of a side-line. Would your reply to this be that in radiesthesia there is no such thing as a 'side-line'? Might I suggest that perhaps we might attempt to bring this more into accord with orthodox medicine by quoting the use of colour by qualified psychotherapists and then going on from there? Very muddled way of putting it, but surely there *is* this link? Have certain colours certain definite frequencies? Are there colours that are malignant? Colour—poetry—and legend. A vast theme.

It is indeed a 'vast' theme. How vast, I was not to realize until I received his reply:

Answer:
About music and colour one must beware of thinking in these watertight compartments. Colour is implicit and inseparable in all our paraphysical work as a part of a continuous vibratory spectrum which we can only conjecture to extend from infra sound, through sound, through ultra sound, radio, infra-red, light waves, ultra-violet, etc. and beyond

our ken. All vibrations are important at some particular level in the cosmic economy and they are also interrelated.

The idea of colour is without meaning when divorced from the mind perceiving it. Colour may have an adverse effect relative to a person's make-up. Certain colours do have an adverse effect on certain types of cell growth, remembering that colours are very definite frequencies measured in Angstrom Units or millimicrons wave-lengths. The frequencies for colours are too astronomical to conceive and it is usual to talk in terms of their wave-lengths instead.

Mesmer, if he had access to our labs now, would be a happy man presumably, with the technical facilities that are available. He was a man with an ultra modern outlook, even today. In his way, he was an Einstein and very near to being a genius. Unfortunately, he achieved fame before his theories were accepted and I have a feeling that he was a poor technologist.

To return to colour again we consider our colourscope to be the finest form of treatment we can produce but it does require the presence of the patient. It must be remembered that it also incorporates the radionic dials. And who knows just what they are doing? I think they are causing a partial materialization of pre-physical energy which in some way shows elastic qualities akin to that of sound.

And there I will say goodbye to the Box. I do so with mixed feelings. I am glad to be rid of a back-aching job—a job which in spite of all our questions seems to have ended only in a flurry of interrogation marks. At the same time, I leave the Box with a certain regret. I believe that the questions it poses are worth answering and I hope that all this clumsy spade-work may perhaps persuade some writer more qualified and more instructed to dig deeper, and straighter, and maybe to strike a richer vein. For obviously in these territories, still so largely uncharted, there is precious metal for the mind.

'Precious metals.' They are for our next chapter, which, by comparison, will be very plain sailing, though it takes us towards even stranger horizons.

10. MAPS FROM NOWHERE

Shortly before the war I had a fan—not my favourite word but it sums up the relationship—whose name was Mrs Nicolaus. She was a woman of about forty who lived in a large flat in Kensington. She was much alone, for her husband was a mining engineer, and his business obliged him to spend a good deal of his time in the Congo. She appeared to be a woman of some means, because whenever I wrote anything which particularly pleased her she sent me a large mixed bunch of flowers from a fashionable florist, elaborately selected and tied together, 'ready for the vase'.

These I promptly undid and rearranged, in a pattern more to my satisfaction.

For some years I never met Mrs Nicolaus. It is better for all concerned if authors steer clear of their public. But one day a letter came from her of a type very different from the normal kindly note of congratulation. It was charged with excitement. Her husband, she said, was coming home next week, and she was deeply anxious that I should meet him, in order to witness a certain experiment which he would be making. I should have explained that Mrs Nicolaus was a spiritualist. She did not mention the nature of the experiment but I guessed that it would be concerned with spiritualism. 'I will not describe what I want you to see', she wrote, 'in case you should think it ridiculous. But I do entreat you to make the effort. Will you please come to dinner on any day that is convenient to you?'

So I went. Mrs Nicolaus proved to be very like my mental picture of her—small, delicate and rather elusive, but no fool, with a pleasant twinkle in her eye and a very musical voice. There were some charming things in the flat and a lot of very good Chelsea china. The husband was Kiplingesque —rugged and bluff, with bushy eyebrows. They were, all in all, a happy, normal and most engaging couple.

There were two other guests—a man and a woman.

The man was a square-jawed engineer called Harris who maintained almost complete silence throughout the evening.

The woman was introduced as Miss Evelyn Penrose. She was about my own age, slim and graceful, with pretty hair and keen grey eyes. She was simply and elegantly dressed in black. There was nothing remarkable about her except a sense of extra 'alertness'; she was so vividly alive that you felt her skin might have been charged with electricity. She had a pleasant contralto voice. If I had been asked to guess her profession I should have said that she was a competent director of a fashion house.

We had an admirable dinner, during which the nature of the 'experiment' was not mentioned. Then the two women left us. Nicolaus motioned me to the chair by his side and passed the port decanter.

'Would you call me a queer-looking fellow?'

'Very much the reverse.'

'Or Harris here? Anything odd or spooky about us?'

I assured him that two less odd or spooky individuals it had never been my pleasure to meet.

'Good. Because what you are about to see is both very odd and very spooky.'

Then it came out.

Miss Penrose was a map-diviner, and tonight she was going to give us a demonstration of her powers.

This may be the first time that the reader has ever heard of map-divining; it was certainly a new one on me. And so, before describing the experiment, I will endeavour as briefly as possible to explain a phenomenon that is, by any normal standards, inexplicable. All one can say about it is that unless a large number of hard-boiled business-men are dupes and an even larger number are liars, it appears to work.

Map-dowsing is simply the application of the mysterious gift of water-dowsing to the surface of a map. Instead of searching for water in a field or a desert the dowser searches for minerals on a sheet of paper.

The reader may well raise his eyebrows. Even if he is sceptical about water-dowsing he will probably allow that there may be 'something in it'. Even if he ignores the massive weight of evidence, he will probably admit, however grudgingly, that the actual theory of water-dowsing was not necessarily conceived in Cloud-Cuckoo-Land. After all, the dowser *is* in contact with natural forces; water—actual water—may send out 'radiations', and these radiations may be transmitted to the hands of the dowser. 'It is very odd'—so the sceptical reader might argue—'and not at all my cup of tea. But it is not of itself totally incredible.'

But surely map-dowsing must be totally incredible? How could a map—a piece of paper that has been pulped and processed and put through a lot of whirring rollers—a fragment of vegetable matter that has been dyed and stamped by a number of completely non-human devices—how could such an object send out any meaningful 'radiations'? How could it transmit any 'message' that could possibly have any significance whatsoever?

These questions, which I have assigned to my imaginary sceptical reader, are the questions which I immediately asked myself.

There is a short and snappy answer to them. Miss Penrose made, and still makes, a considerable income from her strange talents. To say precisely how much would be an impertinent intrusion on her privacy, but when I heard, from Nicolaus himself, the fee that she was being paid for her services on this particular evening, I opened my eyes very wide. This income is not paid to her by starry-eyed dreamers but by men who want their money's worth. We will give chapter and verse for this not unimportant fact before we say goodbye to her.

Let us finish our port, walk upstairs, and watch her at work.

She was standing in front of a table under a bright hanging light. The table, which was about six feet square, was covered with a large scale map, about two inches to the mile. A printed map . . . one that had been through a machine. Not a map that had been drawn by hand. This, I think, is important.

There were no names on it, but there were contour lines and areas shaded in different colours. These I took to be indicative of some sort of property divisions. Across the map meandered a big river.

Nobody, so Mr Nicolaus told me, had informed Miss Penrose of the locality of the land which the map portrayed. It might have been a map of an area in Florida or Greenland or New South Wales. Miss Penrose, presumably, being a shrewd woman, had a hunch that it was somewhere in Africa. She was not being given a large fee by these gentlemen merely in order to provide me with an evening's amusement.

'What do you want me to look for?' she said abruptly.

(Mrs Nicolaus, by the way, had been banished to another room. Miss Penrose did not care to have women around where she was working. Men were different, indeed, sometimes they stimulated her, especially if they were musical.)

'What do you want me to look for?' she repeated.

They told her. Copper and silver.

'I'm glad it isn't oil.'

All this was so strange that I found it impossible to keep silent. 'Why are you glad it isn't oil?'

'Because when I'm looking for oil—or rather when I *find* it—I feel positively filthy. As though I were covered with the stuff. I have to go and have a bath.'

All this in the most matter-of-fact tones.

She reached for her bag. 'Have you told Mr Nichols what this is all about?'

'In very general terms.'

'Then let us come from the general to the particular.'

Out of her bag she drew something which at first I took to be a charm bracelet. Then I saw that it was a thin circle of wood from which dangled an assortment of jewels and metals.

She held it out in front of her. 'This is a diamond. This is virgin silver. This is raw copper.' And so on.

She delved again into her bag, and drew out a little ball hanging from a chain. 'And this is my guide and mentor. This tells me where to go, by the way it swings. I take down its instructions on the map with a pencil.' She gave me a quizzical smile. 'Is that quite clear and simple?'

Instantly she answered her own question—I can hear it over the years—'*It is either simple or it is nothing.*'

I asked her a last question. 'Does this take a great deal out of you?'

'You mean . . . is it exhausting? That depends. One's reaction differs according to what one is looking for. Oil is certainly exhausting. But most metals merely communicate by tempo.'

'What do you mean by tempo?'

'I suppose you could call it the rhythm of the vibrations. However, there is one thing that might amuse you. About silver.' She transferred her smile to her employers. 'I think you ought to give me a bonus when I look for silver.'

'Why . . . silver?'

'It tickles.' She gave a wholesome, full-throated laugh. 'It pricks and stings and itches. Like plunging one's hand into a bed of nettles. Yes, I certainly think I should get a bonus for silver.'

She turned back to the table. The smile faded. Suddenly she became a dedicated person.

'And now, let us warm up the map.'

Her thin delicate fingers raced over the parchment like the fingers of a pianist. Now we were all quite silent. I thought of her phrase 'It is either simple or it is nothing.' Well, if you could accept the fact that there was magic at work it was very simple indeed. To her, the map was *alive,* it was emitting some form of vibration, and she was tuning in to these vibrations, adjusting herself to the same wave-length.

She took up the piece of crude copper, and with it the ball on the chain. In the other hand she held a pencil. She started at the top of the map. The ball did nothing. Then over to the left. Still nothing. Then she came down towards the centre, towards the river. And suddenly the ball started to swing. As it did so she marked the reactions on the map.

I leant forward and studied her hand very carefully. It was as steady as a rock; there was no sign of even the flicker of a movement. I suppose that a skilled manipulator could cause a ball to swing sharply backwards and forwards without appearing to move his own fingers . . . or could he? But even if he could, what would be the point of it? In particular, what would be the point of it to *her?* She was not doing a parlour trick, she was fulfilling a business engagement.

This went on for several minutes. There was now quite a complicated pattern of pencil marks on the map, in a roughly triangular area, most of it in the vicinity of the river.

Suddenly, the ball stopped swinging.

She let her hands drop to her sides. 'That's all I can do about copper for the time being.' She stared at the pattern she had traced. 'Does it mean anything to you?'

Nicolaus glanced at his chief engineer. 'It certainly does. It means a lot.'

'Good.' She put the piece of copper back on the wooden circlet and detached the fragment of raw silver, which she laid on the table. Then she went through the motion of wringing her hands, as though she had just dipped them in water and could not find a towel. She turned to me with a smile, still shaking her hands vigorously. 'Do you know why I'm doing this?'

'I can't imagine.'

'Copper sticks to one's hand. I'm shaking it off. To start fresh on the silver.'

'Like cleansing your palate before tasting a new wine?'

'Precisely. You're getting the idea.'

She bent over the map again. This time she 'warmed' it very quickly. She went through the same motions of holding the silver and the ball in one hand and a pencil—this time it was a red one—in the other.

Somehow—and here I may be indulging my fancy but I think not—the atmostphere in the room seemed lighter. As though the change from the heavy copper to the bright sparkling silver was in some way communicating itself to us from the surface of the map. At any rate she was smiling.

Suddenly, she gave an involuntary exclamation as though she had pricked her finger. The ball swung quickly. 'Here it comes,' she murmured. 'It's terribly ticklish.'

Once again she traced on the map the area the ball was indicating. This time it was on the other side of the river, sometimes right down to the banks, and unlike the copper, which had been in one distinct block, it appeared to be distributed in narrow streams. Every so often her hand twitched —I remembered her simile of the nettles—and once the reaction was so intense that she flinched as though she were in actual pain. Shortly after this she stopped.

She held out the hand which had contained the silver. 'Feel that.'

I took hold of the fingers. They were so hot that she might have been holding them in front of the fire.

'I told you that I ought to get a bonus when they make me look for silver.'

Nicolaus and Harris were bending over the map. On their faces was an expression of considerable satisfaction.

'Are you happy?'

'Very.'

'Judging by the behaviour of my little friend'—she was putting the ball back in her bag—'you're on to a good thing.'

'That's what we believe too.'

We went upstairs for a night-cap. She did not stay for long. When she said good night to me she repeated that strange and meaningful sentence: 'It's either simple or it's nothing.'

The sequel to this story—if it can be called a sequel—came in my final conversation with Nicolaus and Harris. They told me that the patterns she had traced on the map were almost precisely identical with the findings of their geologists. They had employed Miss Penrose because a good deal of capital would have to be sunk in the two enterprises before they could expect a profit. They had wanted to make assurance doubly sure. Well . . . now they had their assurance. They were going ahead.

This was an isolated episode in my life before the war, and the outbreak of war was the only reason why I did not, for the moment, follow it up. The war, too, was presumably why the idea formed in my mind that Miss Penrose was dead. After all, a great many of one's friends were, and one had been pretty near it oneself, on more than one occasion. And then, twenty years later, Miss Penrose suddenly came into my life again. I was in a train, reading a weekly review, when my eye caught the headline 'Gullibility Unlimited'. It proved to be an attack on Evelyn Penrose who, it seemed, had just published a book called *Adventure Unlimited** in which she described her travels round the world as a diviner. The writer was very sarcastic; his technique of criticism consisted of quoting sentences out of context and sometimes misquoting them. Thus:

Green Fingers. 'Watch the phosphorus stream from my finger tips!'

Corpses. 'I have no wish to turn myself into a human bloodhound!'

Gold. 'One has to get up early!' †

---

* Neville Spearman, 1958.

† This was a particularly misleading paraphrase. The passage in the book which prompted it runs as follows: 'One of the most trying things about prospecting for gold by divining is that one has to start work at sunrise. Unless one does, instead of getting the reaction for gold over the actual vein or alluvial deposit, the rays seem to become deflected, and one can get as many as twelve "phantom" places or mirages, not one of which is over the actual gold deposit, although it may give the diviner all the required reaction. This is a difficulty which is experienced by practically all diviners.'

But it was the critic's caption to 'Silver' that caught my attention. This time he quoted her verbatim, presumably because he thought the whole idea so supremely ridiculous.

Silver on the ground gives the diviner a strong and often painful reaction; it is like being stabbed through the feet and body with a red-hot knife. The first time I went over a silver mine in Canada I thought I had trodden on a rattlesnake.

I get the same reaction from a map.

But I had *seen* this very phenomenon with my own eyes! I had seen those sensitive fingers twitch and flicker over the map, as though they had been stung by nettles. And I had seen them in circumstances which seemed to preclude any suggestion of fraud, against the respectable background of a Kensington flat, under the scrutiny of two very sober business-men.

When the train reached London I took a taxi to the ancient establishment of Messrs Hatchards in Piccadilly and told the driver to make good speed. I bought the book. I read it far into the night. I got in touch with Miss Penrose's publishers, who informed me that letters should be sent to her, care of the Bank of Adelaide, Perth, Western Australia—an address which sounded pleasantly reassuring, as though it brought her down from the clouds into the normal commerce of everyday life—exactly the sort of address which I should have wished her to have. Because I wanted to talk money.

One of the main troubles about books which deal with psychic matters is that their authors seldom consider the economic facts of life. One reads of healers with astonishing gifts, of seers who can apparently pierce the veils of the future, and one is tempted to ask 'Why are not these people millionaires?' They cannot all be of such an ethereal disposition that they would resent making a little on the side. (As it happens, there does seem to be general consensus of opinion that when psychics work for *purely* mercenary reasons they 'dry up'. The magic leaves them. And we have already seen, in the case of Harry Sanctuary, how sharply he resented a light-hearted suggestion that he should use his pendulum on a race-card.)

However, the nagging suspicion persists. That is why I plucked up my courage and wrote to Miss Penrose, care of that solidly respectable address. I was still tingling with excitement from the marvels in her book, but I wanted this extra assurance. I wrote as follows:

Your book tells of a life-time in which you seem to have been working miracles. I have seen one of these with my own eyes. Your gifts are the more impressive because they have so often been harnessed to commercial purposes. Can you give me chapter and verse, facts and figures . . . in short, signed testimonials? I am making this request for a very good reason. You are among those who have 'lifted up their eyes unto the hills'. If we can persuade the sceptic that whatever else you may have seen in those hills, you saw gold, and caused men to dig for it and find it, the man-in-the-street may be inclined to give more heed to the message implicit in the body of the book, which is of course a spiritual one.

I received the testimonials by return of post. We will examine them without delay. Having done so we shall be able to read the rest of the astonishing Penrose story as fact rather than fiction. Which makes a difference.

The Minister of Finance in the Province of British Columbia is presumably a respectable person. We may assume that he does not prepare his budgets merely by gazing into crystals. The Attorney General of the Province may be granted a similar character, and so may the Minister of Mines and the deputy Minister of Agriculture. If all these four gentlemen got into the witness box, of their own volition, and announced To Whom It May Concern that Miss Penrose had performed these miracles in their Province under their very noses, the most sceptical critic would sit up and take notice.

Well, that is precisely what these four gentlemen did.* Their testimony deals with her work in Canada over a period of several years, not only in finding water but in prospecting for minerals and oils—sometimes on the spot, sometimes *from a map*, sometimes at a distance of thousands of miles.

* I should mention that these particular testimonials are dated at various periods in the early 'thirties. Whether the present heads of government in Canada would endorse them I do not know. In any case, the precise date does not seem of much importance.

Ministers of State do not indulge in ecstasies, particularly on such controversial matters, in which public money is involved. But they went as far as they could.

Thus—from the Minister of Mines: 'The tracings Miss Penrose made over a map of the Cariboo district when she was using her pendulum in my office *coincided exactly* with the information received from engineers in the district under whom operations are being carried on.'

'I bespeak for her a hearing,' demanded the Minister of Finance. The Attorney General described her work in water-divining as 'very satisfactory'. He added: 'She was also asked, while employed on this work, to check up possibilities of oil being found in a certain section of the Province. It is to be noted that her reports *entirely agreed* with the views of geologists who had been employed in checking up the strata in this section of the Province.'

The Department of Agriculture was equally enthusiastic. 'Having personally accompanied Miss Penrose on both water- and oil-finding trips I am in a position to vouch for her outstanding ability.' Most significant of all was the fact that solely on her advice, drilling and digging operations were initiated and that 'many satisfactory reports have been received after sinking the wells'.

That is only one sample, among a great many, of recognition on a governmental level. In spite of the sober language in which the tributes are expressed, the facts to which they bear witness are none the less astonishing. If a sensation-mongering journalist on a Sunday newspaper had got hold of them he would have been justified in using the biggest type in the building for these headlines.

For example:

AUSTRALIAN WITCH DICTATES CANADIAN POLICY
MINISTER OF FINANCE HYPNOTIZED BY PENDULUM
GOVERNMENT BY NECROMANCY

Apart from the word 'witch'—though I have a fondness for witches—one may ask whether Miss Penrose would have any cause for taking legal action against such statements or whether, with her saving salt of humour, she would have wished to do so. For in her modest way, she *did* 'influence Canadian policy'. And though the Minister of Finance might cavil at the word 'hypnotize' he was so impressed by that pendulum that he—rightly—followed its instructions.

From all over the world these tributes have flooded in.
An oil tycoon from Michigan wrote:

Only God knows what talent or ability or gift she
has. All I can say is that the whole thing is very remarkable indeed, considering that *she was on the other side of
the world* in Australia when she made this survey, and
to my knowledge has never been within a thousand miles
of Michigan and has to this date never met myself.

He had good reason to pay tribute to her. She located no
less than twelve oil wells for him!

From a tin-mine in Cornwall came this tribute: 'You told
us that after the second seam we should find disturbances
and faults which would destroy the wolfram contents of the
lode. This is exactly what did happen and on your advice we
have stopped developing.'

From a colliery in Burton-on-Trent the managing director wrote: 'She had never been in the district before and
was provided with an ordinary six-inch Government Ord-
nance Survey plan of the neighbourhood. With extraordinary
precision, and without the smallest hesitation, she indicated
on this plan the line and direction of a big fault, which was
known to us. She then explained that it thickened to the
north and probably split at a point which she indicated. This
proved to be the case.'

Many of these testimonials express the bewilderment of
those who employed her. The managing director of a gold-
mine in British Columbia wrote:

I must confess that I do not understand it at all. Had
I drawn the survey myself, *after* having seen the veins
and sampled them, I could not possibly have found it
more accurate.

I could fill the next ten pages with similar tributes. Perhaps
the most heartfelt comes from an Australian farmer who
was saved from bankruptcy after a long period of drought
by the same swing of that little pendulum *over a sheet of dry
paper*. 'I consider her map-work bordering on the miraculous,' he wrote. 'It is an unparalleled triumph. I am confident that from now on we shall have all the water we need.'
He did.

Why has this extraordinary woman never been given the recognition which is her due? True, she has received substantial material rewards, which she certainly earned. But why have none of the hundreds of men whose business careers she forwarded had the sense to see that in these matters they were in touch with powers of unlimited potentialities? Miss Penrose is not the only map-reader in the world. She is a virtuoso, but she is not unique. Why is map-reading, to the average man, a phrase that means nothing at all?

And why did her book make no sort of a sensation? Why wasn't it front page news? Why should *I* be the first to make a fuss about it?

Your guess is as good as mine.

Maybe the reason is fairly simple. Map-reading is magic and there is no M for Magic in the files of the world's newspapers. A reporter who came back with a story about magic would probably be told by the news-editor to kill it, or to palm it off on to a woman's magazine. But that is not where this story belongs . . . though I am the last person to say a word against women's magazines. This story deserves to be told from a higher platform.

But what *is* map-reading? The question is the more urgent because we now know, after all this spade-work with the testimonials, that it 'works'. Obviously, the best person to answer the question is Miss Penrose herself. She will do so in the next chapter.

11. ECHOES FROM THE EARTH

Wonder at all things before you, for wonder is the beginning of knowledge.

THE OXYRYNCHUS PAPYRI

We are just entering what may be called 'the field of vibrations', a field in which we may find more wonders than the mind can conceive.

MARCONI

In the last chapter we gave an eye-witness account of Evelyn Penrose at work, finding minerals *on a map* when she was thousands of miles from the areas in which they were located.

In order to assuage the reader's incredulity—and our own—we collected a body of testimony to the effect that for the past thirty years her life has been devoted to this practice, and that her gift has been responsible for the expenditure of large sums of money, sometimes at Government level, and large profits for those whom she advised. Whatever else the reader may or may not believe in this book, he is obliged to believe *that*. This testimony is at the disposal of any responsible person who cares to scrutinize it. Miss Penrose is not a braggart but she has no desire to hide her light under a bushel. She believes in that light; she believes that in its small way, like a slender taper, it might help to illuminate some of the darkness of the modern world.

But we are still a very long way from discovering how it is 'done'. When I ask myself this question my mind immediately gets cluttered up in a tangle of words. *Words*—those chipped, tinkling, tarnished and utterly inadequate tokens which we are obliged to employ in our eternal efforts to express the inexpressible. Words like 'vibrations', 'telepathy', 'radiations', 'pre-cognition' . . . none of them worth a halfpenny.

So where do we go from here? I think we look into Miss Penrose's mind. After all, she also had to use these wretched words, when she wrote her book. She does not always use them with expertise; she is not a professional writer; and throughout her life she has probably been animated by the principle that the pendulum is mightier than the pen. And yet, though some of her theories might be more clearly expounded, something 'gets through', and it is something very much alive.

Listen to this:

A water-map is much less exhausting to do and needs a different technique. After 'tuning-in' my map and making it alive, I ask 'it'—whatever 'it' may be—questions and instruct 'it' to tell me where the water-sheds are. I only use a survey-plan and not a topographical map but, if there are any hills from which the streams are coming, a *strong draught* comes up off the map and *lifts my hand on to the high land,* after which my hands float gently over the map, showing me the direction of the streams from the water-shed. The little pendulum then outlines the course of the underground streams with the most minute accuracy and I draw them in. Before the map is finished, the depth must be added to each stream and a test made for the potability of the water.

If it were not for the aforesaid testimonials—and all the money which they represent!—we might be inclined to dismiss this as a minor episode from the Adventures of Bluebell in Fairyland. But we cling to those testimonials.

We also cling to a word in the last sentence, the word 'potability'.

This is a most remarkable word, in its context. I cannot believe that it was put in for effect. What it means in the plainest English is that you can *taste a map.* 'Potability', she says, 'can be tested in several ways but, both on the ground and on the map, my lips and tongue taste salt if the water is brackish, and I get a horrible smell in my nose if it is sulphurous or impure.' This is a conception so bizarre, so far from the common rut of human experience, that it carries its own 'aura' of truth. To taste a map is extraordinary; but would it not be equally extraordinary for a woman of Miss Penrose's background to invent the *idea* of tasting a map? This is the sort of grotesque mental somersault that one finds in the nightmare prose of Dali. It is pure surrealism. I cannot see Miss Penrose as a surrealist.

Before we leave this section we might pause to observe the use of the word 'it'. Once again we seem to be confronted by the X Force. Perhaps Miss Penrose is wise simply to call this force 'it'. Elsewhere she confesses: 'I have no more knowledge of what the force or emanation to which I "tune" in is than I had when I was a child. I do not even know what to call it, which is the great difficulty in writing about divining.'

The surrealist parallel runs all through her comments on map-divining; they carry conviction by their very unlikelihood. Thus: 'When I am dealing with a rich mineral deposit, say wolfram or copper, I am so violently thrown and tossed about that I feel like a doll on a piece of string.' Every mineral, it seems, has its own special 'sensation'. I was particularly interested in her remarks about oil, because they confirmed my own memory of our conversation thirty years ago.

If I am looking for oil and my hands rest immobile, I know that there is no oil there. *If my hands are over oil they start to rise alternately.* Where the oil is very rich, my arms and hands are thrown back with such force that I think they would be torn out of their sockets if I were not double-jointed. All this is done with my eyes shut. Working on an oil-map is an extremely exhausting performance and one can only keep at it for about half an hour. My assistant then takes the maps and numbers the area according to the violence of my reactions and lightly pencils in my remarks.

From time to time, in these unique and sometimes almost frightening records of the manner in which natural forces flow through her, she pauses and allows herself a moment of philosophical reflection. Her observations, at such moments, are simply spoken but they are strangely impressive.

I sometimes wonder whether the ill-effects on diviners when seeking oil is Nature taking her revenge for their interference in her work which she carries on secretly in the earth. If it is true that oil is still in a state of metamorphism, it seems possible that if it were left undisturbed in the earth it might eventually become drastically changed and possess powers about which, at present, we can only surmise.

Even now, no one wants oil for the actual oil itself but simply for the power it already contains and which man has learnt to release for his own use and mis-use.

In spite of my work as a diviner which includes the

finding of more oil, I cannot but admit that perhaps the world would be happier and its future less gloomy if oil, and the extraordinary power it contains, had never been discovered.

We have already noted—some readers may think too frequently—the 'aura of virtue' which seems to surround those whose lives are devoted to the practice of radiesthesia, in one or other of its forms. Miss Penrose has this aura in a marked degree. Like Dr Michael Ash, whom we met in our first chapter, she believes implicitly in the positive power of the Lord's Prayer. To her it is a sword to draw against the powers of darkness.

> When one is alone and unprotected one's greatest protection lies in reciting the Lord's Prayer out loud. It should be said again and again, *without a break,* as the ritualist Mantras of the East are recited, and its power over the forces of evil is very great.

She is modest about her gifts. She wants others to share them, as she thinks they can; she believes that the divining faculty—at any rate where water is concerned—is more widely disseminated than people imagine, and that this faculty can be so developed in most of us that it will enable us not only to locate the existence of water but to determine its depth, its volume, its quality, and the precise direction in which it is flowing. (She is referring, of course, to work *in situ,* not to work on a map.) She even gives precise instructions as to how we can exercise these latent powers, by standing on a fallen tree, holding a pendulum in our right hand, 'using our left hand and arm as antennae, stretched out with the first finger pointing in a straight line with the arm'. She then describes what is likely to happen, and gives us a sort of code with which to interpret the various movements of the arm and the pendulum, at the end of which she observes: 'Which, I am sure everyone will agree, is very easy.'

And always, as we have seen, she has this extraordinary and instantaneous reaction to what might be described as the 'personality' of the minerals with which she is in contact. Oil makes her feel as though she were walking through a thick fog, tin gives her a sensation of exhilaration, gold and diamonds are the 'practical jokers' of the diviner's world, causing him many disappointments, 'perhaps', she says, 'to punish him for foolishly investing them with a fictitious value'. But the worst of all is pitchblende (the matrix of radium) or any substance that is radioactive. It induces a 'scorching red-hot pain'.

Here, perhaps, there might be material for the sceptic, which I am only too ready to hand him, for I may well have seemed over-credulous in the foregoing pages. 'Is it not possible', he might ask, 'that Miss Penrose may have given the game away in that phrase which you have quoted about her feeling for gold and diamonds? You tell us that she is a virtuous person, which we are prepared to grant. And obviously to many virtuous people gold and diamonds are the symbols of Mammon. Might she not, therefore, be unconsciously influenced by this moral attitude when she is actually looking for them? Might she not say to herself—even if she does not say it in so many words—"I am looking for things of which I do not really approve, things which the world would be better rid of?" Might not this moral attitude dictate the swing of her pendulum and moderate the movement of her hands? Might this not be especially evident in her reaction to pitchblende? Might not the horror of *any* sensitive person to the thought of the H-Bomb cause some sort of "scorching" reaction?'

Here the sceptic has a point, and I should like to think that these pages might encourage some more competent writer to develop it. Evidently, in this mysterious affair, we have to take into consideration some form of telepathy, even if it is only 'self-telepathy'—to coin a phrase that is almost, but not quite, meaningless. (After all, if we can hear the echo of our own voices, is it not conceivable that we might also catch the echo of our own psychic personalities?)

Where the sceptic's argument falls down, I would suggest, is in his assumption that Miss Penrose knows, in advance, what she is looking for. Sometimes she does, sometimes she doesn't. She may, on occasions, have a sort of roving commission to discover whether there are *any* precious metals in the vicinity. Such a commission might well begin with a search for gold, in which she would employ the technique of the pendulum with the sample of raw gold attached. But whatever her code of ethics, or however strong her moral convictions, she would obtain no reaction from the pendulum unless gold was actually in the soil.

The whole business is a vast and, to me, almost painfully

exciting detective story, with clues that reach from the bowels of the earth to the most distant stars, with the hounds of heaven chasing round in magic circles, snuffing up the scent and getting their noses powdered by gold-dust. In the centre of it all stands a small, feminine figure, holding out her arms, swinging a pendulum.

And—with a swift descent to bathos, for we surely need a touch of it—bringing in the cash. Without that cash, without those testimonials, without those heart-felt letters from oil tycoons, coal merchants, sheep farmers, attorney generals and such-like lucky people, the whole of the Penrose Saga would be a fairy tale. As it is, we must accept it as a record of fact.

Which reminds me that I have a great liking for fairy tales—reading them and writing them. In the next chapter I shall tell one. I hope that it will not be the less readable because it happens to be true.

12. GREEN FINGERS

The secret Strength of Things
Which governs thought, and to the infinite dome
Of heaven is a law, inhabits thee.

SHELLEY

The Divinity within the flower is sufficient of Itself.

MAY BRUCE

I have never been able to understand why the phrase 'old wives' tales' should have a derogatory interpretation. Surely, if any legends are to be believed at all, they are the legends handed down by wise old women, in tales that have been told and retold throughout the centuries?

No tale—even if it is a fairy tale—stands up to the test of time unless there is a germ of truth in it. No phrase—even if it is a magic phrase—gains universal currency unless it is founded on fact.

Consider the phrase which we have used for our title. The origin of 'green fingers', with its variation of 'a green thumb', is lost in the mists of history. We shall never know who said it first; all we know is that it is as old as the art of gardening itself. Moreover, it is in universal circulation and has its counterpart in every language. In France they speak of *le doigt vert;* in Germany it is *der grüne Daumen;* there is even a version in Japanese, which is perhaps not so surprising when one remembers the Japanese love of gardening.

All this has a significance deeper than is generally realized. For the phrase 'green fingers' is a magic phrase, indicating a supernatural phenomenon. If it does not do that it indicates nothing at all. It drops to the level of a piece of foolish whimsy which would never gain general acceptance, nor stand up to the test of time. The world may not have realized that it is magic, and a great many gardeners who have actually used the phrase might be startled, and even displeased, if you told them that by doing so they had affirmed their belief in supernatural phenomena. But it would be interesting to hear the arguments with which they would deny this affirmation. They would not be very impressive.

Of what nature is this magic?

Presumably, it must consist in some form of 'radiation'. And if the people who run our lives had a grain of sense, they would stop spending multi-millions on devising new methods of blowing us all up, and would start spending the money on something sensible—like paying ten thousand housewives to sit in greenhouses stretching their hands over pots of geraniums. I did not write that for a laugh. If ten thousand housewives were actually paid to sit in greenhouses stretching their hands over pots of geraniums a great deal of knowledge—green, growing, wholesome knowledge—might be added to the store of man's wisdom. We might at last begin to learn something about the subtle and exquisitely delicate relationship which exists between the animal and the vegetable kingdom. We might be able to assess, however faintly and tentatively, the common creative denominator between the sap in the limbs of an oak and the blood in the veins of a man.

As a gardener and as an employer of gardeners I had long accepted the theory of 'green fingers'. But only since the study of radiesthesia have I been able to interpret it in a way that seems to make sense. Till then one had merely used it as a convenient catchword, as though one had gone through life saying 'Abracadabra' without realizing that 'Abracadabra' had a magic significance.

I knew that I had green fingers myself, that I could do things with cuttings that other people seemed unable to do, and that when I transplanted certain trees and shrubs which, after a certain age, are usually regarded as untransplantable, they flourished. Such as a ten-foot *Buddleia alternifolia* which had no fibrous roots at all. But I attributed these successes—if I thought about the matter at all—to the fact that I knew more about gardening than some of my contemporaries. And also, perhaps, that I spent rather more money and took rather more trouble. And cared more. A tree out of the ground, with the sacking round its roots, bleeding its life out, affects me almost as profoundly as a kitten mewing at a desolate back door when its owners have gone away. I ache for it, and with it. I even talk to it, when the occasion demands. I do not see why one should not talk to trees. They are beautiful; they have authority and wisdom. And in the very nature of things you are obliged to talk *up* to them. You can never 'talk down' to a tree. And they are wonderful listeners. To most of life's problems they have a multitude of melodious answers.

The reader will not, I hope, imagine that I go about patting the trunks of blasted oaks and telling them that they are poor little oakey-pokies but that daddy will soon put them right again. All that I am trying to indicate is that I have always had a very strong sense of a rapport with things that are green and growing, and that instead of neglecting this sense I have tried to cultivate it. To revert to the oak tree. If you actually embrace an oak tree, and throw your arms around its trunk, you may look very foolish, but—since all matter, even dead matter, gives out radiations—you will be setting in motion a chain of radiesthetic reactions which will do neither you nor the oak tree any harm.

Let us now put these theories to a practical test by visiting one of the most extraordinary gardens in the world.

It lies in a secret corner of the Cotswolds, and if you had seen it as I saw it, on that hushed and thundery evening, though you might have responded to its charm you would have been puzzled as to why anybody should describe it as 'extraordinary'. We will come to that in due course. Meanwhile, try to imagine a rambling, neglected garden, wandering under ancient trees through over-grown hedges . . . a garden that might have been the setting for the second act of *The Sleeping Beauty*. A hushed and solitary place—solitary but not lonely, for one had a curious sense that it was haunted. The word 'haunted' is of all words in the English language one of the most evocative; it has an echo in it, a whole chime of echoes that ring down the corridors of one's mind like the echo of voices in an empty building . . . haunted . . . haun . . . ted. Most of these echoes, in our current pronunciation of the word, have a timbre of sadness. But here there was no sadness; indeed, there was great happiness and an abiding peace.

I was standing staring at one of the most remarkable horticultural phenomena I have ever seen in thirty years of gardening. It was a clump of *Campanula latifolia*. This is an amiable flower, related to the Canterbury bell, which is a stand-by in many suburban gardens during the latter half of June. Pale-blue, modest, shyly drooping its head, it seldom reaches a height of more than three feet.

But this extraordinary campanula had shot up to a height of *nine* feet. To make sure that I was not dreaming, I had stepped up to it and lifted my arm over my head. At least nine feet, maybe nine feet six. Moreover, everything about it was to match. You could scarcely get your fingers round the stems. As for the flowers, they were a brilliant, almost truculent blue. You might say that you could almost *hear* them chiming. Indeed, I do say it. I have always felt that colours can be heard, if one listens properly, that there are, for example, combinations of green and grey that have a sensory connotation with the music of muted 'cellos. Wilde was not being so foolish when, in *The Picture of Dorian Gray*, he made Lord Henry ask his hero to 'play something scarlet by Dvorak'.

For a long time I had heard of the experiments of Miss May Bruce, and her theories of compost making, but she had always remained a rather vague figure in my mind. Some people described her as a fanatic and others as a saint. But there were many others who swore by her methods—including the agricultural correspondent of one of our greatest national newspapers.

And so I decided to make the journey to see her and to hear her story . . . because there was one aspect of this compost that seemed very apposite to the investigations which we are making. Miss Bruce claimed that the vital principle of her activator was *radiation*.

I will try to give this statement the dramatic impact that it deserves by drawing a picture.

Put the clock back to a summer morning twenty years ago. Imagine the figure of Miss Bruce moving about in an ancient toolshed whose shelves are lined with bottles. These are filled with the juices of living plants—dandelion, nettle, camomile, yarrow, valerian and many others. There are also infusions of oak bark and jars of honey.

It is an important morning in the life of Miss Bruce. During the night she has had a dream. There have been many nights when she has tossed and turned, feeling blank and lost, fearing that all her work would come to nothing. Last night was very different. 'I woke up in the morning', she was later to write, 'with the key of the problem in my mind and the words ringing in my head: "*The Divinity within the flower is sufficient of Itself.*" '

This dream, to her, had only one interpretation—that life

came from life, and that all the vitality needed to strengthen the life of plants could be extracted from other plants. There and then, she began to experiment with her juices, feeling, as she confessed, not unlike an alchemist weaving spells in a medieval laboratory.

At last, after many trials and errors, the solution is ready. And now the picture really does become dramatic. She stands there, in front of a row of jars filled with lawn mowings, chopped-up weeds, nettles and general vegetable matter, all waiting to be treated. But one all-important question remains to be answered. In what proportion should the solution be used? How is she to ascertain the right strength?

Well, she was no scientist, and there was nothing for it but practical experiment. And so:

> I treated the contents of the jars with the solution in the following strengths . . . one in ten, one in thirty, one in sixty, one in a hundred. And then, urged by an impulse, *one in ten thousand*.

Miss Bruce, as I was to learn, is convinced that the 'impulse' which caused her to make this extraordinary and apparently nonsensical decision was dictated by a psychic control.

You can probably guess the end of the story. The jars were carefully labelled, mixed, and placed with their labels to the wall. She wrote:

> Within five days the contents of one of the jars had gone ahead and was changing colour rapidly. After ten days I invited a soil expert to come and see the progress of the experiment and place the jars according to their merit. When he had made his choice, we turned them, label forward, and then read:

> First.   One in ten thousand
> Second. One in a hundred
> Third.   One in sixty.

We all have our own ideas of what constitutes drama. To me this quiet and rural episode is essentially dramatic. For though you may dismiss the 'dream' of this very truthful and honourable lady, and though you may scoff at her 'impulse', and though you may attribute her astonishing decision—to use her extract in such microscopic proportions—as a sort of homeopathic fluke, you are still faced with the hard commercial facts of the sequel.

For the fame of Miss Bruce's activator, and the stories of the magical effect it was having on the compost heaps in her garden, spread far and wide. And a great many important people began to wend their way down the shadowy lanes that led to her old rambling home. And Miss Bruce began to find that she was likely to make a great deal of money.

But she did not want a great deal of money. Not for herself, at least. She had the little that satisfied her needs, which were simple enough—to live among things that were green and growing, to make them grow greener and grow stronger, and at the end of the day to sit in the garden and listen to the song of the birds.

So she gave her secret to a great commercial firm, whose managing director happened to be, as she was, an idealist. Today you can buy it on the market, where it competes with conspicuous success against a vast array of products with the same pretensions. Whether it has quite the same potency in its mass-produced form, I do not know. I have the feeling that there may have been a special personal magic in that old lady's fingers, and that conceivably *some* of the magic may have been lost in the inevitable hurly-burly of commerce, though it remains an exceptionally powerful fertilizer. For I can never forget the sight of those campanulas, those electrifying flowers surging up to the sky from their bed of lusty compost,* singing a song of praise in a shade of electric blue.

Throughout this book we have endeavoured to relate the miraculous to the commonplace. In discussing supernatural occurrences we have not forgotten the economic background against which they took place. To reinforce the phenomenon of map-divining we collected testimonials from businessmen and government servants in high office. When we come to discuss 'spirit-healing' we shall approach the subject through the doors of a respectable chartered accountant in the City of London.

Can we offer similar evidence to prove the efficacy of Miss

---

* A practical exposition of Miss Bruce's methods of compost making has been published by Faber & Faber, 1943: *From Vegetable Waste to Fertile Soil* by May Bruce, 3s.8d. post free. This is a book that can be given to any jobbing gardener, written as it is in down-to-earth prose, with no psychic frills about it.

Bruce's compost? I think we can—in my own garden. To the majority of readers this claim may seem not only pretentious but impractical for the purposes of our argument, particularly to Americans, who can hardly be expected to hop on to a jet and fly to Europe in order to measure the height of my campanulas. However, it does happen to be a fact that in my present garden this compost plays a very large part. It is also a fact that since the publication of a book I wrote about this garden,* thousands of visitors have come to inspect it. These visitors, almost without exception, have found it difficult to believe that the garden could have been created in so short a time. They have stood under trees that surely must have been planted twelve years ago, and when I told them that they were, in fact, planted only *four* years ago they have smiled politely and changed the subject. So often has this happened that in sheer irritation I had a poster printed on bright pink paper, giving the facts, figures, and dates of the various plantings. This poster I pinned to the walnut tree with drawing-pins, but obviously most people do not believe it.

But it is true, as you may see for yourself, if you care to make the effort. Not for one moment would I suggest that this exceptional burgeoning and blossoming has been entirely due to the fairies tinkling their magic wands. To no small extent it is due to Mr Page, the gardener, who is a prize transplanter, and to my own efforts with the hose on the long hot nights of summer. But I am convinced that there has been another force at work. I have been gardening all my life, but not until my present garden was I aware of the existence of this method of making compost. And not until my present garden have either I or Mr Page been so constantly astonished by what goes on. Blue poppies almost up to one's shoulder (*Mecanopsis baileyii grandis*), bigger, bluer, and better than any in the Savill Garden, which is the Mecca of blue-poppy lovers. Hostas with such enormous leaves that when I see the same plants in other people's gardens I cannot resist the temptation to inquire, with heavy sarcasm, whether theirs is a 'miniature' variety. Clematis that are clambering over the roof when, by all the rules and regulations, they should scarcely have topped the window of the music room, etc., etc. These plants are all open to inspection, and the thousands of gardeners who have inspected them will not complain that my account has been exaggerated.

* *Garden Open Today* (Cape, 1963).

The compost heap is also open to inspection. After the foregoing superlatives this may come as something of an anticlimax. It looks very like an ordinary compost heap; it is not brewed in a witch's cauldron, and if you approach it towards the hour of dusk, you will see no ghostly figures hovering over the pile of lawn-sweepings, cauliflower stalks, withered leaves, mildewed carrots, straw wrappings of old champagne bottles, slime from the pond, potato peelings and old copies of the *Daily Telegraph*. But if you care to prod into it, and dig your fingers into this mélange, you will find that it is *not* an ordinary compost heap. For all these incongruous and often unsavoury elements have been blended by Miss Bruce's magic formula into a fragrant union, rich as chocolate, sweet as honey. (Pure run honey was one of the essential ingredients of her original recipe—one small drop of it.)

The compost, in short, has an exquisite *smell*, even if you happen to pick a lump which was originally formed from the malodorous slime from the pond.

I feel almost ashamed to revert to that 'aura of goodness', which we have noted on so many previous occasions; the reader may suspect that this is a sort of theatrical prop, like a battered halo, which is dragged out of the cupboard when the going gets hard, in order to explain various phenomena which are otherwise inexplicable. We must risk that criticism. But let us raise the argument to a level higher than the sort of thing you might expect to find in a popular magazine under 'Jottings of a Sentimental Gardener'. We are trying—are we not?—to relate a rotting cauliflower stalk to the abiding harmony and sweetness of the universe. We are standing in front of a lot of muck, staring at it, marvelling over it, wondering what is in the heart of it. Deep, deep down in the heap, the X Force is working in that cauliflower stalk, on that slime from the pond, on the withered leaves, even on the soggy slips of the *Daily Telegraph*. Making them smell sweet. How? Why? We need a poet to answer that question and maybe the poet is Browning, with his passionate belief in the essential virtue that lies hidden in the heart of man.

> There is an inmost centre in us all,
> Where truth abides in fullness; and around
> Wall upon wall, the gross flesh hems it in
> This perfect, clear perception—which is truth.
> A baffling and perverting carnal mesh

Binds it, and makes all error; and to *know*
Rather consists in opening out a way
Whence the imprisoned splendour may escape
Than in effecting entry for a light
Supposed to be without.

For 'wall upon wall' we might read 'layer upon layer'—
for 'perverting carnal mesh' we might substitute 'rotting vegetable matter'—and we might compare the 'truth abiding in
the inmost centre' with the mystic power of the X Force
radiating through the whole heap, escaping into the sunshine
from which it came, mingling again with the good earth,
climbing through root and branch to the last leaf of the tall-
est tree—and then, failing again when the sunlight fades, in
an eternal cycle of life and death and renaissance.

However you may regard such speculations you may perhaps agree that they make gardening more exciting. And—
all speculation apart—my *Mecanopsis baileyii grandis* are
almost shoulder high.

Inevitably, the pioneers in these fields of infinite acreage
have 'gone back to the soil' at one time or another, as though
they wished to reassure themselves by the cool contact with
the earth from which all things stem. In a contemporary
pamphlet about Mesmer, published in Paris shortly before
his death, there is a story that he would interrupt his baquet
sessions to stride over to the flower border, dig his fingers
in the soil, and recharge them with some universal essence. A
lifetime of research would be needed to explore the thoughts,
theories, dreams and experiments of the many men and
women who have sensed this 'terrestrial radiation' and have
endeavoured to interpret it—and maybe it would be a life-
time well spent. An anthology of the men whose souls have
met the soil, and learned from it, united with it, been healed
or distracted by it, might make fruitful reading. I have neither
the time nor the temperament for such an undertaking. However, we might extract a few documents worthy of consideration.

Under the letter S in my cluttered files we find a good deal
concerning Rudolph Steiner (1861-1925) who was greatly
concerned with these affairs. Steiner is a difficult figure to
'place' in the history of radiesthesia. He was obviously a genius, he was something of a saint, and he inspired almost fa-
natical devotion in his followers. The proof of this devotion
is evident, in concrete terms, in London's Rudolph Steiner

House, and in a number of other institutions scattered all over England, where his spirit is very much alive.

Steiner was a great believer in the influence of the moon on the growth of plants. This belief, as we have seen, is widely held among peasant folk all over the world, and crops up again and again in folk-legend. But Steiner gave it a new twist. He claimed that the power of the moon made itself felt largely through the medium of *water*. Speaking in 1924 to the Agricultural Course of Koberwitz he said:

> Water contains far more than what emerges from it chemically in this process [electrolysis], as oxygen and hydrogen. Water, in fact, is eminently suited to prepare the ways within the earthly domain for those forces which come from the Moon. Water brings about the distribution of the lunar forces in the earthly realm. There is a definite connection between the Moon and the water in the Earth. *With the forces that come from the Moon on the days of the Full Moon something colossal is taking place on Earth.*
>
> We shall therefore have to consider the question: Is it not of some significance whether we sow the seed in a certain relation to the rainfall and the subsequent light of the Full Moon, or whether we sow it thoughtlessly at any time?

There are not many 'Steiner farmers' in modern Britain, and even fewer in America. But the limited number who follow his principles are so enthusiastic that their methods seem worthy of wider attention. They can be studied in *Star and Furrow*, the journal of the Bio-Dynamic Agricultural Association.* This is a modest sheet with a limited circulation but it contains much food for thought. For example, in the latest issue that lies before me, we may read the testimony of certain modern German farmers who sprinkle their seed-beds with what they call 'Full Moon Water', collected from a few minutes before to a few minutes after the time of the Full Moon. They claim that the results of such methods are spectacular.

Eccentrics? Even lunatics? None of us, perhaps, can answer that question until a great deal more research has been

* Further particulars from the Secretariat, Broome Farm, Clent, Stourbridge, Worcestershire, England.

undertaken, though in this matter of the full moon we might perhaps find it significant that here, once again, we catch the echo of the voice of Mesmer. And even when that research *is* undertaken we must be prepared for shocks. Many are the stories one collects, as one goes along, concerning the relationship of plants to men, and of men to plants. In one of our questionnaires to de la Warr we have already noted the curious figure of the Reverend Franklin Loehr, who 'cursed' a plant for five weeks until it died. Mr. Loehr's energies are usually more kindly directed. He is a member of the Religious Research Foundation of Los Angeles, where for some years a number of experiments with plants have been carried out under—so I am informed—the most testing conditions, in a spirit of devout sincerity. Before me lies a photograph of Loehr sitting beside two pots of lima beans. The pot on the left, over which he had prayed, shows plants of vigorous growth, over a foot in height. The pot on the right, which had not been given what Mr Loehr describes as 'the prayer boost', shows plants that are thin and stunted.

What I am trying to stress, in these random paragraphs, which should be regarded only as rough notes for some writer more competent to tell the final story, is—as far as the garden is concerned—the vital interplay between mind and matter, fingers and foliage, men and plants. In the tensions of modern life we are all too apt to forget this interplay. Ideally, we ought to be able to stand under a giant oak and *be* the oak. We ought to be able to say, without any fear of a guffaw from the gallery: 'I am you, and you are me.' We ought to be able to feel its sap in our own veins and to be quietly confident that our own blood is flowing through its branches. In moments of true illumination we ought to be so aware of this that any suggestion to the contrary would be unthinkable. The oak's music, as the wind sighs through the branches, should be our music, transcribed in the same eternal rhythm, written on the same immortal staves.

Very seldom do most of us find ourselves in the right place to do this—the right mood, the right 'weather', to indicate the general climate of the spirit. If we are all diviners, in a greater or lesser degree, as would seem to be the case, we are distracted by countless physical and mental influences . . . pylons striding across the horizon, scarring the cornfields with their hideous limbs of steel, radio sets buzzing in near-by houses, like angry bees, to say nothing of the swarming fears and frustrations of a thousand neighbours, laying waste their lives in a ceaseless rhythm of getting and spending. And so, when the oak stretches out its arms in welcome we cannot see, and when its leaves whisper their music we cannot hear.

Here I would like to indulge in a moment of pure fantasy. Is it altogether too far-fetched to suggest that just as there are evil men and women so there may be evil plants and flowers? The human race contains all too many examples of parasitic personalities and poisoned minds. It is currently fashionable to attribute these twisted natures to social frustrations, economic hardship, lack of education. I am not so sure. A really exhaustive statistical survey of evil might knock holes in this argument. Why is it that the average sensitive man shrinks insinctively from most of the toadstool family? Why does he avert his fingers from them? Why to even the untutored mind do they appear as symbols of disease and death? Few 'flowers of the forest are prettier than a group of fly-agaric (*Amanita muscaria*) clustering under a beech tree, their skins toasted to a golden brown, like cakes that the fairies have been baking, delicately spotted with a design that might have been fashioned out of spun sugar. These, and the even more poisonous death-cap (*Amanita phalloides*), abound in our woods through the last weeks of summer, asking to be plucked and nibbled . . . woods which are explored by thousands of children. No notices are nailed to the trees to warn the public that death is waiting in these woods, in the most attractive guise, and few parents, even if they think of such matters at all, are qualified to advise upon them. And yet, although there is enough poison in our native forests to slay by the thousand, deaths from mushroom poisoning are very rare indeed; in fact, during the whole of 1963 not one was recorded. The logical explanation would seem to be in the fact that fungi like the destroying angel (*Amanita virosa*) give out a 'vibration' of evil, of which children are perhaps even more conscious than adults. To dimiss this as a fanciful aversion is hardly an example of the scientific approach. Aversions and prejudices, rational or irrational, affect the rise and fall of nations. The Second World War was sparked off because an evil lunatic set a match to the smouldering fires of anti-Semitism. Maybe this particular form of beastliness has some radiesthetic interpretation. I would not put it past the de la Warr Box to sniff out an anti-Semite in disguise.

However, this is taking us too far from the original subject of our inquiry—green fingers. Let us put this to a practical test by enlisting, once again, the services of the extraordinary woman whom we have met in a previous chapter . . . Evelyn Penrose, map-diviner.

It is hardly surprising that Miss Penrose has the gift of green fingers developed to a remarkable degree. And since she is the last person to claim exclusive talents, and has an almost childlike belief that others might follow in her footsteps if they would only try, she has laid down precise instructions telling us how we may prove whether our fingers are 'green' or not. She writes:

Very few people know that 'green fingers' is a phenomenon visible to the naked eye, which can be seen by almost anybody.

The simplest way to test it is to hang up a dull black cloth on a door and stand with your back to the light which should not be too bright. Then hold out your hands close to the black cloth, with the palms towards you and the fingers spread out, your hands being about an inch apart. Then look at your fingers in a dreamy way, as if you were looking at a distant landscape through a window with your thoughts far away. Let your eyes be slightly out of focus.

The first thing that you will see will be a steadily thickening mist round the tips of your fingers, from which a phosphorescent ray will emanate. Then put the fingertips of both hands close together without touching, so that the rays of both hands mingle. The hands can then be slowly drawn apart and the rays stretch like a piece of elastic. If the hands are stretched too far the rays will break, but it is easy to start again and re-join them. When the 'green-fingered' experimenter can do this, he can turn his attention to sick trees and plants.

Were it not for the fact that we have already quoted convincing testimonials to the effect that Miss Penrose is a woman whose word is to be trusted even when she makes far more remarkable claims, we might be inclined to dismiss this strange exercise as a piece of wishful thinking. When I first put it to the test myself, I was convinced that I saw this 'mist' on several occasions. Indeed, I was so certain of it that I introduced the subject into a lecture which I was giving in various cities of the United States, demonstrating the technique on the platform. Not surprisingly, I received a great many letters from members of the audience, informing me that they too had made the experiment and that they had seen the 'mist' quite distinctly. However, I do not seem to possess the faculty today, however hard I try. Possibly I am trying *too* hard, and am too anxious for proof that is absolutely positive. It is right to be on one's guard against self-deception, but to force oneself into a mood of incredulity is as foolish as to drift into a mood of indiscriminate acceptance. Miss Penrose tells me that we must look at our fingers as though we were 'looking at a distant landscape'. I have trained myself to be so on the alert against other people's tricks and one's own illusions, that I find this very difficult.

13. CLOSE-UP OF A HEALER

I must begin with a good body of facts and not from principle, in which I always suspect some fallacy.

CHARLES DARWIN

In the collection of facts one cannot be over-cautious. But in the invention of *theories*, especially in a field so peculiar as ours, where analogies drawn from the existing sciences are almost useless, a canny and sober circumspection would be the greatest mistake.

PROFESSOR H. H. PRICE in his
Presidential Address to the Society of Psychical Research

Suffolk Lane, in the heart of the city of London, is not a spooky thoroughfare. If it were to conjure up any ghosts at all they would be Dickensian—seedy clerks hurrying down the stone staircases of the narrow buildings on their way to the Circumvention Office, pale-faced widows knocking on the doors of cobwebbed chartered accountants, shady individuals drifting up from the riverside for a pennyworth of gin at the Coach and Horses round the corner. Some of these characters, *mutatis mutandis*, are still to be encountered, but the clerks are no longer seedy, the widows may be attired in pale-blue trousers, and the gin costs two and sixpence a nip.

As for the cobwebbed chartered accountants, no description could be less fitting for the immaculate figure of Mr F. Hagley, senior director of the firm of Hagley & Knight, to whose offices our footsteps are now directed.

My object in calling on Mr Hagley was very simple. Spiritual healing, particularly the work that centres round the figure of Harry Edwards, is now 'big business'—the term is used in no derogatory sense—and I wanted to prove that it was also honest business. I had no personal need of this assurance, but what of the general public? When the man-in-the-street finds himself held up in a traffic jam outside the Albert Hall, when he sees long queues of patient people stretching round the block and way into the distance, in the hope of buying tickets of admission, and when he learns from the posters that these people have gathered here in order to witness a 'Demonstration of Spiritual Healing by Harry Edwards' he may well ask himself: 'Where does all the money go?' In fact, he *does* ask this question. Often, in my discussion of the powers of Edwards, I have heard the words: 'He must be making a pretty good thing out of it.' I have even heard them in Harry's centre of healing, the Sanctuary at Shere. They came from a rich old woman who had consulted him about her arthritis, and she spoke them as she rather grudgingly deposited a ten-shilling note on his collection plate, which was roughly ten per cent of the sum she would have paid—and had very frequently paid—to a Harley Street specialist.

Hence the visit to Mr Hagley, perched in his Dickensian eyrie with its view of the distant Thames. For it was Mr Hagley who had gone to Shere in his professional capacity, had subjected a cross-section of Harry's immense correspondence to hours of careful scrutiny, and had then given his written testimony that the letters did in fact exist and that they appeared to be 'quite bona fide'. I wanted to hear this from Mr Hagley's own lips. Well . . . I did.

I also wanted to learn rather more about the whole financial set-up. Without betraying any confidences Mr Hagley left me with the impression that this 'big business', as far as its finances and its general operations were concerned, was conducted on ethical principles, with no suggestion of any attempt to defraud the public, nor any desire to do so.

'But if you ask me what is actually happening,' he added with a rueful grin, 'what power is at work, what it all means, you'll have to apply to some other department. All I know is that the people who wrote those letters obviously *thought* they were cured, and maybe to think you are cured is the next best thing to being it.'

Which seemed to me a sensible observation.

Admittedly, this is not a very sensational story . . . so far. It only becomes sensational when we study the letters themselves, reading them, perhaps, with a deeper interest because of Mr Hagley's certificate. For if they are true, as they appear to be, the fact emerges that tens of thousands of people all over Britain, indeed, all over the world—people who are not deranged nor notably eccentric—are at least *under the firm impression* that from this Sanctuary in a quiet Surrey backwater there has come a force of healing which has radiated through their own bodies, curing them of every known disease, and in many cases bringing them back from the brink of death.

Even if these multitudes are literally deluded—though why we should presume to call them so is not apparent—the *fact* of their 'delusion' is one with which any honest doctor, or any honest sociologist, should be prepared to reckon.

Before going any further we should perhaps define our terms of reference.

When these matters are discussed at dinner parties—I choose dinner-table conversation to typify the rather casual and transitory nature of society's interest—'spiritual healing' and 'faith-healing' are used as though they were interchangeable terms. They are not; they are in no way connected; indeed, they might almost be regarded as antipathetic. Perhaps that is going too far; faith, obviously, could not be a negative influence in any form of therapy. But it is essential to realize that faith—at any rate as far as the patient is concerned—is not and never has been a necessary element in spiritual healing.

The simplest proof of this lies in the fact that a large amount of spiritual healing takes place *without the patient being aware that he is under treatment*. The very nature of the healing is the reason for this odd state of affairs. Many sick people are suspicious, hide-bound, locked in their own despair. Some, it is true, will grasp at any straw, but others, who have worn out the heels of their shoes tramping up and down Harley Street, are so fatigued and disillusioned that they would regard a visit to a spirit-healer as the final insult. Thus it comes about that their wives, or their relatives, or their friends go behind their backs and arrange for them to be put on what is called 'absent treatment'. As the weeks go by they note a gradual improvement. They hold their breath and cross their fingers, until a day arrives when the improvement is so marked that they feel justified in confessing to the patient that he has been on the list of Harry Edwards, or whoever the healer may be. Even so, the reaction is not always what they might have hoped. I know one chronic arthritic who was so infuriated by the discovery that he had been cured, as it were, by stealth, that he threatened to institute divorce proceedings, naming Harry Edwards as a sort of psychic co-respondent!

I have sat with Harry Edwards, and his two principal colleagues George and Olive Burton, while this 'absent healing' was actually going on, and a very strange experience it was. We gathered round a table on which was piled a heap of unopened letters from all over the world—enough to fill a large sack. Before we began Harry suggested that we should have a minute's silent prayer. But my mind was wandering; I could not keep my eyes off those letters, remembering the sum of human agony that they represented, the burden of physical pain. If we had been silent for long I should have found the tension difficult to bear; many of the envelopes were addressed in scripts so twisted and crippled that they seemed to scream out for immediate attention.

Then they began to open the letters. For the most part there was silence, but from time to time one of the others would pass a letter to Harry for his special attention. Usually, when they did this, he would close his eyes, holding the letter in his hands, and then passing it back without comment, but sometimes he would scribble a note on his pad for future reference. There was a curious mixture of business efficiency and religious devotion; at one moment one might have been in a city office, at the next in a church. The letters were swiftly opened and swiftly read—how could it be otherwise with so formidable a collection? But in spite of the speed of the operation, the concentration of the healers on each letter was intense. Even the almost illegible scrawls on some of the air-mail letters from abroad were subjected to a sharp 'ray' of attention.

And here is an interesting point. At one stage in the proceedings I asked if I might be of assistance in opening a few of the bulkier envelopes and passing on a précis of their contents. (Some of the communications arriving at the Sanctuary are as long as a novel by Dostoevsky and twice as painful.) The answer to this offer was a gentle smile and a shake of the head. I gained the impression that this would in some mysterious way 'disperse the energy' that was being generated; there had to be actual physical contact between the paper on which the letter was written, the fingers of the healer, the brain of the healer, the spirit of the healer, and . . . what?

The X Force?

Before we attempt to answer that question, let us open a few of the letters,* remembering that they have as worthy a

---

* These letters are chosen from over *ten thousand* cited by Harry Edwards in *The Evidence for Spirit Healing* (Spiritualist Press, 48 Old Bailey, London, EC4). This was first published in 1953. Since then the movement has greatly extended, and it may be assumed that today there are at least a quarter of a million persons who have benefited—or believe they have benefited—from spirit-healing.

certificate of authenticity as we could reasonably demand.

If miracles can be monotonous, then the ensuing paragraphs will be monotonous indeed. For each one bears witness to a miracle. And each one uses the actual word . . . 'miracle'.

Let us begin with the bitterest scourge of all . . . cancer.

Lewis. The specialist tried hard to find any trace of the cancer. His own doctor made an examination and then said: 'Go to chapel and thank God for the miracle that has been done to you.'

Gavers. When the doctor saw my wife's serious condition he called me into the surgery and after expressing sincere regrets confirmed the presence of a growth with the words: 'There is no hope.' A month later she visited this same gentleman and the wonderful improvement amazed him. He really could not believe his own eyes. To him it was a miracle. He then said that the trouble was removed and it certainly would not return.

Bellis. I lost my post as the doctor considered I could not get better. On a further examination the surgeon found the growth, which was malignant, had left no trace at all and he considered me to be in very good health. In the hospital my recovery was considered miraculous.

Andrew. The miracle has happened. The obstruction suffered by Jean suddenly cleared, when a natural motion took place. The doctor was astounded at the complete change in her condition.

Arthur. My very grateful thanks to you for my husband's miraculous recovery. The surgeon who operated for cancerous growth told me there was a feeble chance of his coming through. The surgeon also is astounded at his progress.

Dempster. The second X-ray, taken last week, was found to be negative. The sister told her husband it was a miracle.

Durnin. The cancer research specialist has told her she is a case in a million. He gave her two weeks to live —eight months ago. He says in his forty-five years of cancer research she is the first patient to prove him wrong when he has said the case was hopeless. She was

a mass of cancer and according to the hospital authorities the cancer was even in her bones. It is a miracle.

These are seven cancer cases, chosen almost at random,
from several hundred. Since the day when they were published the cases have multiplied into several thousands.

When I was a young reporter Sir John Bland-Sutton, who
was then President of the Royal College of Surgeons, told
me that in his opinion the wickedest men in the world were
those journalists who, for the sake of a good story, published
sensational accounts of cancer 'cures' which had not been
properly proved or authenticated. 'Time and again', he said,
'I have walked down hospital wards on the morning that one
of these "cures" has been announced; I have seen the almost
rapturous expression of relief on the faces of patients whom
I knew to be incurable, and I have had the heart-breaking
task of disillusioning them.'

I thought of those words when quoting the cases above. I
fervently agree with them. But surely there is another side to
the picture? If these cases I have quoted, and thousands of
others of a similar nature, are in fact genuine, would it not
be equally wicked of us not to give them credit and to learn
as much as we possibly can about them?

The stock objection of the medical profession to spiritual
healing, particularly in the case of cancer, is that the healers
do not supply the patients' medical history. When confronted
by some cure which they are unable to explain they take
refuge in the excuse that 'there must have been some mistake in diagnosis'. In other words, the patient never had cancer at all, nor tuberculosis, nor arthritis, nor whatever the
disease may be. They have even gone so far as to refute the
identity of X-ray photographs.

To this objection Edwards makes the following reply:

When doctors have considered our healing work in
the past, they have generally and rightly asked for the
patients' medical history. *This we can rarely give.* The
reason for this is that we have to deal with the patients
themselves, or their friends, to whom the doctors will
not release the official medical history. The only information that we receive is from the patients' letters
which describe the symptoms and what they have understood their doctors to say. *Any attempt of ours to obtain a sight of an X-ray, or to obtain any information* ..

from a doctor or a hospital has failed. Even when we have asked the patients, or their relatives, to obtain any information, it is only very rarely that it has been given, and then orally. Many times we have asked: 'What does your doctor say?' and received the answer: 'He does not tell me anything.'

This refusal of the medical profession to co-operate, however much it may retard any general recognition of spiritual healing, does not seem, in fact, to make much difference in the actual results. With disarming frankness Edwards observes: 'As we have not received any medical training, a medical case-history would not be of any assistance.' With equal frankness he adds: 'If any medical authority wishes to investigate any of the cases cited, we can supply the correspondent's name and address; and from the information they can give about the doctors who attended them they should be able to obtain the patient's history.'

Would Sir John Bland-Sutton, confronted by such evidence, and such an attitude, have classed Edwards with the sensation-mongering journalists whom he so rightly despised? Would he have extended his strictures to include myself? I hope and believe not.

In these pages it would be superfluous to call any more evidence as to the reality of spiritual healing, which appears to operate with equal effect through the whole domain of disease, in all its manifestations. For years this evidence has been available to the general public, and it is reasonable to suppose that if any of it had been false it would not have escaped the attention of the medical profession, even if it had passed the keen eye of the chartered accountants. With a minimum of trouble they could have nailed a thousand lies and sent Edwards scuffling back to the obscurity from which he should never have emerged. But they have not taken the trouble. True, in a statement issued by the British Medical Association in 1956 we find the admission that 'recoveries take place that cannot be explained by medical science', but it was made by the average doctor, who prefers to go on mixing his potions and sharpening his scalpels.

Personal Note. This chapter is not going to be totally non-critical; there are some aspects of spiritual healing which puzzle and disturb me; and in the next section we shall examine them.

But before we do that I should like to draw attention to

an aspect of the actual *technique* of the healing of cancer, as described by Edwards, which seems to me to have a strange and rather macabre ring of truth. It appears that one of the reactions, constantly noted after healing has begun, is 'an exceptionally heavy rectal discharge, of so unusual a character and large in quantity as to indicate that the mass of the growth has been disassociated from its anchorage and emitted from the body.' The evidence of this phenomenon is clearly set forth in Harry Edwards's book, and it is not unreasonable of him to suggest that 'here surely is a case for medical co-operation, for the stool to be analysed to see if its contents are akin to cancerous matter; and, if so, to ponder on how it is that the cancer with its infiltrations can be separated from the rest of the body to be so completely discharged.'

This is a grim passage, in more senses than one. But perhaps there may be other readers, equally untutored in medicine, who may share my feeling that it seems to carry conviction. Edwards did not invent the phenomenon, the record is wide open for inspection. To me it sounds like our old friend, the casting out of devils. And at least it is something that, emotionally, I can understand.

But there are other things that I cannot understand, even emotionally, and these things we must now consider.

In two very vital respects spirit-healing—at least as it is practised by Harry Edwards—diverges sharply from all the other manifestations of what we have called the X Force.

Firstly, it is publicized. Some of its most sensational operations—and some of its most remarkable cures—are conducted under the bright lights, on the platforms of great buildings like the Albert Hall, in the presence of thousands of spectators.

Secondly, it is 'personalized'. By which we mean that Edwards, not content with regarding himself merely as a channel through which the X Force seeks expression, has given to this force 'a psychic habitation and a name', or rather two names—Pasteur and Lister. He insists that these two eminent ghosts are inspiring his spirit and guiding his fingers.

In due course we will ask Edwards himself to explain this conviction, which he holds quite honestly. For the moment it is enough to note that it is of fundamental importance. Whenever we have seen this force at work we have observed that it seemed to demand, for the full manifestation of its powers, conditions of tranquillity and concentration. True, Mesmer had his sessions round the baquet, but they were limited to a very few patients, and these patients were literally bound together by silver cords emanating from the 'magnetized' contraption in the centre, and an atmosphere of the most intense concentration was induced not only by the hypnotic personality of Mesmer himself but by the whole set-up; the dim lights, the fragrant censers and, on certain occasions, the music off. Apart from this one exception the force seems to demand solitude and intense 'pin-pointing' of thought. If we take water-divining as the simplest and most obvious example we shall perhaps remember Professor Maby's contention that the force is easily distracted and 'dispersed', particularly by human emotions. 'A person in a state of emotional disturbance', he told us, *'bumps the ether.'* So it was with Miss Penrose and her pendulum; she would not even have another woman in the same room. All forms of telepathy, as we shall later note, demand conditions of almost monastic quiet and contemplation; and throughout our long and tortuous examination of the Box, one of the few principles established beyond contention was that the *thought* of the operator, pin-pointed on a blood-spot with intense concentration, was an essential element in the whole technique, perhaps *the* essential element. For that matter, when I assisted at the opening of the letters during the session of absent healing with Edwards himself, this 'pin-pointing' was one of the things which struck me most forcibly . . . that and the silence, and the sense that each written communication was being subjected, as it were, to an individual 'radiation'.

Perhaps we could cross out the whole of the last paragraph and substitute for it eight simple words that have echoed down the ages like an incantation: 'Be still and know that I am God.'

But how can you be 'still' at these great public meetings, which play so important a part in Edwards's campaign to spread his healing gospel?

Consider these great public rallies at such places as the Albert Hall. I have no doubt whatever that his main purpose in holding these rallies is evangelistic. And I should be the first to admit that they are often superbly presented. The addresses are moving and sincere, the music which follows them is exquisitely played and sung, the lighting is contrived with the greatest artistry . . . in short, we have here an example of religious showmanship in the highest degree. And why not? If we are to object to showmanship, *per se,* we shall quickly find ourselves quarreling with a great many activities of the Roman Catholic church, for Rome is surely the greatest showman of them all.

But how is all this to be reconciled with the spirit we have called the X Force? How can you make yourself into an immaculate instrument of this mysterious power under the bright lights? True, Harry Edwards seems to be able to do it. I have seen him perform miracles in precisely these torturing conditions. But I always felt that he was performing them 'against the stream'; that they were only accomplished by a Herculean effort of will-power. When it was all over he gave me the impression of a great actor exhausted after playing an exceptionally arduous role. I may be quite wrong, and he would probably tell me so. He *may* be getting strength from his spiritual patrons, Lister and Pasteur. Or he *may* be absorbing into his own body a tremendous surge of corporate energy from the crowds who watch him. Indeed, this type of energy, akin to that which is generated at a Negro revivalist meeting, is perhaps the most likely source of power on these occasions.

All the same, whatever the explanation, it would seem to be a type of energy fundamentally different from the X Force.

And now for Lister and Pasteur.

In his book *Spiritual Healing,** Harry Edwards gives an account of the manner in which these two persons were made manifest to him. For fifteen years, he tells us, he had been sent to act as an instrument for spirit-healing without knowing, or seeking to know, the identity of the 'guides' who were using him. However, as time went on, he began to receive through his spiritualistic contacts a number of descriptions of spirit personalities of various nationalities who had been 'seen' working through him. Naturally, his curiosity was aroused, and in March 1946 he approached a well-known medium, Mr. Frank Leah, with the object of obtaining more precise information.

Leah was co-operative, but at first he was conscious only of 'group influences'. However, as the weeks went by, these influences merged into two definite personalities, and at length, in May, he received through clairaudience the names

* Jenkins, 1960.

of Pasteur and Lister. At this point another well-known medium, by name Paulette Austen, comes on to the scene. At a séance on May 4th, when six people were present, Mrs Austen beckoned to Edwards to tell him that she was clairvoyantly seeing spirit people associated with him. She first described a bearded man who was a surgeon possessing great powers of concentration. He was of French nationality. His work was connected with glandular research and microbes. Animals were associated with this work and the medium saw a chimpanzee, kittens and dogs. She also described a laboratory where there were wheels, scalpels and test-tubes. She said the letter 'P' was before her eyes, and then rapidly followed the statement: 'He was responsible for finding the cure for rabies.' Then she wrote the name of Pasteur.

Mrs Austen continued: 'There is a second personality and he is much stronger with you—he is your principal healing guide. He also was interested in animals and research concerning them, especially with the study of gangrene. He is of this country and was a surgeon as well as a great research worker. He was also a lecturer. This one works more with you than the first one. On earth they worked on similar lines, and though they lived in the same period they never met. They now work together with you and the first one [Pasteur] is more interested in research for the study of cancer and brain disorders. He is further carrying on work now concerning the nerve bases and spinal and brain diseases.'

At this point Mrs Austen broke off, wrinkling her nose and looking round her and saying that she could smell something like disinfectant. She went on: 'The second one is your main guide, and it was he who found a way of preventing gangrene and of putting people to sleep.' After a few seconds she added: 'I get the initials W.T.L., and I am impressed with the name of Lister.'

A few moments later Mr Leah went over to his easel and in the presence of Harry Edwards made a rough sketch of the head of a man, indicating the shape of the forehead and the outline of the eyes, the nose and the mouth. On Edwards's return home he consulted the encyclopedia, and was convinced that the sketch was that of Lister.

A few days later he paid a return visit to Leah, who completed the sketch—again in his presence, and again at great speed. The sketch bore a striking resemblance to the photograph which, apparently, Leah had never seen before. It is published as a frontispiece to *Spiritual Healing,* and though it is hardly a work of art, it is certainly a striking likeness.

The reader's reaction to this explanation will depend upon his temperament. The sceptic might feel justified in regarding the whole story as suspect. He could point out that anybody with a slight talent for portraiture, who had access to a public library, could produce facsimile likenesses of Lister—or of Beethoven or Crippen if it comes to that—without having access to any exclusive sources of spiritual information. The briefest perusal of any summary of his career in a dictionary of biography would have been enough to have given Mrs Austen all the information she needed. I have mixed feelings about the story myself, inasmuch as it does not seem to have that instinctive 'ring of truth' which we have sometimes detected when we were examining other supernatural phenomena. At the same time, in justice to all concerned, I think that the sceptic should be prepared to provide a *motive* for this remarkable story before he dismisses it as false. There was certainly no financial motive, for no money was involved. Moreover there was not the faintest reason for either Leah or Mrs Austen to stage a fraudulent demonstration, at any rate for the benefit of Harry Edwards. It would have been a mere waste of time, for they would have been preaching to the converted.

But may it not have been wishful thinking, on the part of three devoted disciples, confronted by mysteries so tremendous that they felt obliged to bring them into the compass of a common understanding? May not Harry Edwards have been unconsciously plagiarizing Voltaire, who observed that if there had not been a God, it would have been necessary to invent Him? May he not have felt obliged to *assume* the existence of some such guides as Lister and Pasteur, and, having made the assumption, to believe in it as a fact?

This is really at the heart of the matter, and it is so vital that I have been at some pains to persuade Edwards to put his philosophy into words that the average man can understand. After numerous interviews and a good deal of correspondence I think I have managed to do so.

In a recent letter to me he has pointed out—and this is essential to the argument—that a decisive dividing line must be drawn between spiritual healing and the energy which on our previous pages we have been describing as the X Force. He observes:

It is surely a great error to assume that there is only *one* force that is the panacea for healing. A different character and quality of force is needed for each individual case. For example, consider the totally diverse natures, causes, and manifestations of such diseases as cancer, cataract, blindness or arthritis, or—if it comes to that—producing a chemical change in the blood of a 'blue baby'. Each of these disorders, disharmonies, disruptions, or whatever you may choose to call them, requires a *specially* characterized 'force'.

So far, so good; we can see what he is getting at. The operative word in the above paragraph would seem to be the word 'specially'. He is, in fact, postulating the need for a 'specialist', as though he were leading us in the direction of a sort of psychic Harley Street. Which is, in fact, precisely what he is doing. He continues:

Every spiritual healing is a planned act, for nothing ever takes place by chance. *Intelligence* is needed to administer or use any force.

So when a so-called 'incurable' is healed through spiritual healing what does it mean? It must mean that the planned act is conducted by an *Intelligence that is superior to that of man*.

It cannot be the healer's mind, for he rarely has any medical knowledge.

The intelligence must be able to discern the cause of the disease, to make its own diagnosis and to prescribe the correct character and quality of healing necessary to effect a cure.

The figure of our ghostly specialist looms nearer; we can see him diagnosing, prescribing, measuring his mixtures; we can almost see him waving a spectral stethoscope.

But before Edwards conjures him on to the stage, he has some startling things to say about . . . God. At least, they sound startling to me. In answer to the question 'What is the nature of this Intelligence?' he replied:

Orthodoxy claims that the Intelligence is that of 'God'. But if this is so, some very perplexing questions arise. Does God make favourable dispensations, overriding His laws of creation, in favour of selected individuals?

Why does He turn a deaf ear to the prayers of His clergy, permitting a little child to suffer in anguish or die? The child has not sinned. And why are so many healings so long-drawn out, taking so much time, if an omnipotent God is responsible? If God *hears* the prayers of His clergy, then He must be a consenting party to the pain of His people.

Whatever else we may say about this outburst, we must admit that it has the 'ring of truth'. It has, indeed, the same sort of spontaneous indignation that we find in Shelley's notes to 'Queen Mab', which might be described as the Schoolboy's Guide to Atheism. Edwards is no more an atheist than was Shelley; but in his approach to the philosophical foundations of theology he seems somewhat superficial. However, if we were to take up the cudgels with Harry over this particular passage, we should have to write another book. So let us bring the ghostly doctors, finally, on to the stage. I quote:

The Alternative.

Healing can only take place within the laws of creation. The administering Intelligencies are God's ministers in spirit, who are obliged to work within these laws.

We call them—our Spirit Doctors, or Spirit Guides.

In the life of the spirit they may have every opportunity to gain extensive knowledge how to manipulate and administer the energies we call the 'healing forces'.

Lister and Pasteur are only two of a very great number of 'doctors' in spirit life, who are using healers as channels through whom they direct the healing forces.

For healers cannot heal of themselves; they have not the 'know-how'. All they can do is to *establish attunement* with the spirit doctors, to receive, transmit, and interpret their 'thought directives'.

If I had not seen the power flow through Harry Edwards's hands into the bodies of the sick, time and again, I might feel inclined to dismiss the foregoing paragraphs as so much spiritualistic patter. If I had not held those hands in mine, sharing their power, while his fingers groped their way through old woollen jumpers, on to twisted spines which miraculously straightened themselves . . . if I had not— somewhat squeamishly!—linked my fingers into his over an

old lady's goitre that melted away, leaving the loose skin to
hang down like a turkey's crop, I should say: 'To hell with
your heavenly Harley Street.' But I *have* seen these miracles,
and many thousands of other independent witnesses can
testify to them. So let us not be too concerned about Lister
and Pasteur. Even if they are phantoms of Harry's own imagination—as I believe they may be—they seem to be doing a
pretty good job.

But if they *are* phantoms . . . what then?
The last person you would expect to provide an answer to
this question is Harry Edwards himself, with his 'personalized' theories of healing. But on my most recent visit to his
Sanctuary he did provide an answer, and though it was obviously incapable of proof, it seemed to me strangely convincing.

Here, without correction, are the hasty notes I made while
sitting in the car after I had said goodbye. To give them colour I may add that while I was writing there was a constant
va et vient outside, with cripples hobbling up the drive, and
little stunted children, and once—a pale figure on a stretcher.

'Absent Healing. *How* does it happen?' Harry echoed
my question. *How?* Then, after he had stubbed out his
third cigarette—he smokes too much—he said: 'These
people who write to me are FOUND.' (Caps because
the verb has 'resonance'. It suggests a searching—a groping out into space.) He repeated FOUND. Again he
said 'How?' as though he were really asking himself.
Then he said—very important, this:
'I think they establish a Thought Terminal in the
spirit world, when they write to us. And we, in our turn,
have our own Thought Terminal, and in that way we
establish contact 'like a sort of divine telephonic exchange'. (Another cigarette.) 'You see, Thought, with a
capital T, is a characterized form of energy.'
And then he said the most startling thing of all.
'You know, I don't attach all that importance to Lister
and Pasteur. They're *there*, of course, and naturally I
respect them. But somehow, I feel that I could get on
without them.'
And so do I.

14. TRAINS OF THOUGHT

A motion and a spirit, that impels
All thinking things, all objects of all thoughts,
And rolls through all things.

WORDSWORTH

If telepathy* were the name of an earthly continent there would be few men rash enough to question its existence, however difficult it might be to find on the map, and however artfully it might evade the attentions of the world's geographers. Compared with the evidence for the vanished frontier of Atlantis, there is an overwhelming body of testimony from those claiming personal knowledge of its mysterious territories; indeed, it would hardly be an exaggeration to suggest that the majority of thinking men and women have had one telepathic experience in their lives, or are at least under the firm delusion that they have had one.

The confirmed sceptic may, of course, insist that all these experiences *are* delusions; and if they were recorded only rarely, and if they occurred only in the lives of the credulous and the hysterical, we might give weight to his opinion. We all know that all men are liars. But why should they all tell this *particular* lie, and why, though they tell it in an infinite variety of forms and details, should it appear to emanate from the same kind of source? To revert to our metaphor of the continent, why should every traveller over the boundless seas of the world catch a glimpse—if only once—of the same sort of coast-line, hear the same sort of voice echoing through the same drifting mist, feel the same ghostly spray on his face?

Let us tell a few stories, and let us choose the sort of story which the sceptic will find difficult to question. We are not interested in the achievements of professional mediums, nor in any phenomena which cannot be verified to the hilt.

* The word 'telepathy', until we later define it more clearly, is here intended to include all forms of paranormal cognition.

And for the purpose of the present inquiry let us allow ourselves a touch of intellectual snobbery, on the assumption
that any form of paranormal cognition, when it occurs in the
life of a celebrity, is more impressive than when it occurs in
the life of a nonentity if only because the celebrity has his
reputation to think about.

The story of Swedenborg and the fire has been often told,
but it has usually been told badly, and at too great a length.
As a result it is in danger of gathering dust on the shelves of
libraries exclusively devoted to psychic matters. I shall endeavour to tell it quickly and clearly.

The facts are as follows:

In the year 1759, towards the end of September on a certain Saturday afternoon, Swedenborg disembarked at Goth-
enburg after a trip to England, where he had been honoured
as one of the most eminent Europeans of the century. On his
arrival he took himself to dine at the house of a prominent
English resident, a certain Mr William Castel. At about six
o'clock, he suddenly got up from the dinner table, and hur-
ried out of the room. When he returned, he was pale and
shaking. He was the bearer of strange tidings. A great fire, he
announced, was raging in Stockholm, and it was spreading
fast. The effect of this news on his fifteen fellow guests is not
recorded, but as Stockholm was *three hundred miles away*,
we may presume that it was startling. He went out again,
and yet again, and each time he returned with fresh details.
The house of one of his friends—whom he named—was already in ashes, and his own house was in danger. At eight
o'clock he went out for the last time. (We are not told the
reason for these constant exits; presumably it was because he
needed to be alone and undisturbed in order, as it were, to receive the news over his 'psychic telephone wire'.) Finally,
shortly after eight, he came back with the news that the fire
was under control, and that it had stopped exactly three
doors from his own house.

That is the story.* What does the sceptic say to it? If the
sceptic is worthy of his salt he will presumably say: 'Prove it.'
Very well. The source of the bare facts I have just narrated

* A fuller account, together with other equally remarkable inci-
dents in the life of Swedenborg, will be found in *Noted Witnesses
for Psychic Occurrences*. Published by the Boston Society for
Psychical Research, 1928.

is a certain philosopher by the name of Immanuel Kant,* and he would need to be a very bold man indeed who would dismiss Kant as a credulous gossip. Moreover, even if Kant had been only a dreamer, on this occasion he was so fascinated by the story that he took the most meticulous pains to check and re-check it, even to the extent of commissioning an English scholar by the name of Green to make the most exhaustive inquiries. As a result he asserted that 'Swedenborg's extraordinary gift is proved beyond all possibility of doubt.'

At the risk of being tiresomely reiterative, even if Swedenborg and Kant had been dupes and liars—which is rather like suggesting that Goethe and Schiller were shady gossip-writers—Kant made so many specific statements of fact in his account of the affair that he would have laid himself wide open to the most scathing derision if any of his details had been incorrect. He told how Swedenborg, on the following morning (Sunday), was summoned to the Governor and closely questioned about the disaster, of which there was as yet, of course, no confirmation. And he told how on the following evening a royal courier arrived with the whole story, precisely as Swedenborg had narrated it.

All these facts, remember, he published to the world only seven years after the events in question. Kant, like Swedenborg, was front page news on the European platform. He was not a little man in a back street telling a story for the diversion of his friends in a beer cellar. He was an intellectual giant, and like all great men he had his enemies, who would have been only too delighted to expose him in any fraud. No such exposure, nor even any hint of it, has ever been forthcoming.

One last word to our sceptic. Just for fun I would like to put this story into modern dress, in order that he may be shocked into some sort of understanding of its impact. Let us assume that the narrator is Schweitzer—one of the few men of our age who might have spoken to Kant in his own language. Very well . . . Schweitzer, sitting in his African retreat, suddenly hears a story which interests him so intensely that he cannot rest until he has assured himself of its truth. The story concerns Lord Russell, and an astonishing incident that occurred to him at his club when he was dining with Einstein. Lord Russell, it seems, suddenly went very pale

* *Dreams of a Spirit Seer* (1766).

over the port and rose staggering from the table, announcing that the Tower of London was burning down. In these days, of course, such tidings could be quickly verified, but we must assume that the telephones were out of order. Anyway, Lord Russell goes on getting up, and exiting, and coming back again with these not uninteresting details. The Tower was burning, the Bank of England was in danger, and a lot of hot bricks had landed on Princess Margaret's Bentley. (She was on her way to open something or other.) All this, remember, in the genteel precincts of a London club. And several hours later, when the switches are in order again, the hall porter hurries in with the news that all these disasters—including Princess Margaret's bricks—had in fact most lamentably occurred, though her Royal Highness, thank God, was unsinged, to the last hair of her tiny head.

This, *mutatis mutandis,* was the story that Kant published to the world. We are assuming that Schweitzer hears it, and having heard it, dispatches messengers of impeccable integrity to verify it. Not that there would be any real need to do so for, within the hour, both Lord Russell and Einstein would have been dragged before the television cameras. But supposing it had *not* happened, is it conceivable that a man of Schweitzer's character would have published it, only seven years later, in order to prove Lord Russell's psychic gifts 'beyond any possibility of doubt'?

I have dwelt at some length on the story of Swedenborg— and admittedly taken some liberties with it, though they were not liberties of fact—for two reasons. Firstly because of the intellectual stature of those concerned, and secondly because of the large volume of extraneous contemporary evidence, which has never been questioned and which is available to any student of their lives and times.

But there are countless other stories of men of similar renown. Consider the case of Lord Balfour. In the whole gallery of British statesmen there have been few men of equal intellectual achievement. His political essays and addresses are informed by a larger scholarship and conceived with a sharper lucidity than anything of Macaulay or Disraeli; and the title of his book *A Defence of Philosophic Doubt* * is in itself a reminder that he was scarcely of a credulous disposition.

* Doran, 1921.

Yet Balfour was a crystal-gazer; moreover, he had no objection to the world knowing him as such, for otherwise he would certainly not have permitted the publication, during his lifetime, of the strange story that Andrew Lang told about him in his introduction to *Crystal Gazing*. Briefly, it runs like this. On a certain Sunday afternoon Balfour and his sister were entertaining Lang at St Andrews, and at five o'clock he borrowed Lang's crystal and took it into his study. Shortly afterwards he returned, looking perplexed, and announced that he had clearly seen in it a woman friend of his, sitting under a lamp. And here an element of precognition enters the story, because he also announced that he would discover whether he had been right or wrong *on the following Tuesday*.

And he did. On the following Tuesday, at a dance in Edinburgh, he met the lady in question, whose name was Miss Grant. He told her that on Sunday at five o'clock she had been sitting under a standard lamp, making tea. He described the dress she had been wearing, which he had never seen before. He added that a man had been sitting by her side, in a blue serge suit. He could not describe the man, whose back had been towards him, but he saw the tip of his moustache.

Miss Grant's natural reaction to this information was to suppose that she had forgotten to draw down the blinds of her room. To which Balfour replied that he did not know whether the blinds were up or down; he was not there, in person; he was at St Andrews.

So where *was* he? Where *was* the author of *A Defence of Philosophic Doubt*? Where *was* the future Prime Minister of England? The only possible answer available to the sceptic is that he was in his study concocting a piece of fiction for a popular magazine. If so, it would seem a curious method of furthering a political career.

These stories, and hundreds like them, have been told before. They have been collected and published in anthologies. But for some reason or other they do not seem to have made the sort of impact they should have done. Why? Because they were badly told? Or because the narrators were so familiar with psychic phenomena that they took them for granted? There may well come a time, in the lives of those who move largely in psychic circles, when they no longer react to such phenomena with the sort of primitive shock which they must have felt when such things were new to

them. A prolonged attendance at séances may take some of
the awe out of the ectoplasm, just as an over-indulgence in
ghost stories may mute the rattle of the chains in the haunted
corridor. Be that as it may, I am still new enough, and doubtless crude enough, to feel the shock.

Thus with Robert Browning, and his golden cuff-links.
Browning was no spiritualist, but he caused his own creation,
Mr Sludge, to admit that there was 'something in it, tricks
and all'. And I have sometimes thought that this concession
may have been wrung from him by his own experience with
those cuff-links.

Here is the story.* The scene was a villa in Florence. Enter
an Italian nobleman, one Count Giunasi of Ravenna. The
Count boasts of his clairvoyant faculties, which he wishes to
display before the celebrated English poet. Has Signor
Browning, by any chance, some little object that he could
hand to him? Some relic, some memento, with which he
could experiment? As it happened, Signor Browning had
just what was needed—a pair of golden cuff-links. They could
not have been more suitable for the occasion; he had never
worn them before, either in Florence or anywhere else; and
he was only wearing them today because his other links had
been lost in the wash. So there could have been no tittle-
tattle about them. They were ideally suited to test the foolish
pretensions of Count Giunasi.

One is tempted, at this moment, to speculate on the sort
of picture which a pre-Raphaelite might have made of the
scene. The long drawing-room with its painted ceiling, the
hot sunlight slanting through the Venetian blinds on to the
Aubusson, the poet leaning forward from his baroque chair,
the exquisitely painted fingers removing the exquisitely
painted cuff-links. But as we are sticking to the facts we had
better return to the authorized version as published in the
Spectator.

Browning handed over one of the cuff-links. The Count
turned it round in his hand, 'sensing it'. Then, looking gravely
into the poet's face he said: *'C'è qualche cosa che me grida
nell'orecchio "Uccisione, uccisione."'* ('There is something
here which cries out in my ear, "Murder, Murder!"')

We quote direct:

* The original version of this was published in the *Spectator* on
January 30th, 1896, when Browning, of course, was very much
alive, and he subsequently confirmed it as 'correct in every particular'.

'And truly,' said Mr. Browning, 'those very studs were taken from the dead body of a great-uncle of mine who was violently killed by his slaves on his estate in St Kilda nearly eighty years ago. They were handed down to my grandfather, who wore them all his life, and when he died they were taken out of the nightgown he was wearing and given to me.'

He continues: 'I may add that I tried to get Count Giunasi to use his clairvoyance to give further details on this termination of ownership' (i.e. the extraction of the links from the nightgown) 'and that he nearly hit upon something like the fact, mentioning a bed in a room. The occurrence of my great-uncle's murder was known only to myself.'

In the telling of this story Browning seems to suggest that this was one of those cases where there might have been 'something in it', but later he withdrew even this grudging admission. 'My own explanation of the matter', he wrote, 'is that the shrewd Italian felt his way by *the involuntary help of my own eyes and face*.'

Is it unduly fanciful to suggest that in this 'explanation' we are confronted by the same mentality which inspired the famous remark about his own *Sordello*? 'When I wrote *Sordello*,' he said, 'only two people knew what it meant, God and the author. And now, the author has forgotten.'

As we come nearer to the present day there is a rapid and formidable increase in the number of eminent witnesses to the facts of paranormal cognition in all its forms. That this is so is largely due to the foundation in February 1882 of the Society for Psychical Research, which was the first body of intelligent and impartial men and women to apply the techniques of contemporary science to the phenomena of Psi—to use a convenient blanket term which is now widely used to describe the psychic in general. They may not have put ectoplasm under the microscope—literally—but this was the general idea. Though they were certainly not 'believers' in the supernatural, it would be equally wrong to describe them as hide-bound 'disbelievers'. No sane men or women devote their lives to scouring the skies with a telescope if they are convinced that the heavens are empty.

Among the many great scholars who have been Presidents of the Society we find names such as Lord Balfour, Professor

William James, Sir William Crookes, Sir Oliver Lodge, Professor Henri Bergson and Professor Gilbert Murray. The only one of these with whom I had any personal acquaintance was Gilbert Murray, and since he was one of my youthful heroes I should like to tell a story about him which, at this point, seems apposite.

In the five brief terms during which my father was able to pay the fees for my Oxford education, I was a very energetic young man. I had hardly set foot in the place before I had published my first novel. In my second term I was editor of *Isis*, and shortly after that President of the Union. As though these activities were not enough to fill in my spare time, I decided to found a monthly review, in collaboration with an almost equally energetic young gentleman called Nevill Beechman, and the enthusiastic co-operation of Leslie Hore-Belisha, who was later to become one of the most controversial Ministers of War that England has ever known. In due course our review appeared under the title of the *Oxford Outlook*, financed by a number of long-suffering parents, aunts, and cousins who eventually got their money back with a handsome profit. The *Outlook*, I like to think, was a cut above the average undergraduate magazine. We could not afford to pay a cent to our contributors, but the first number was starred with such names as John Masefield, Siegfried Sassoon, Charles Morgan, Father Martindale . . . and Gilbert Murray.

Professor Murray was induced to contribute because of his passionate faith in the League of Nations, of which he was then perhaps the most eloquent spokesman in Europe. However the article he sent us was not, in my opinion, up to standard, and so I wrote him a polite letter asking if I might come to discuss it with him. Murray would have been quite justified in telling me to go to hell. Why should one of the world's most distinguished scholars submit his work to the scrutiny of an unknown undergraduate? However, he was not that sort of man. He wrote to say he would be happy to discuss it, and that as he would be dining in Balliol on the following evening, he would call to see me at ten o'clock.

When Leslie Hore-Belisha heard about this he asked if he could come too, not only because he had written our opening manifesto—a superb piece of youthful rhetoric—but also because he was going through a brief but intense 'psychic phase' and he saw in the meeting an opportunity of putting Murray to the test. I should explain that Murray had recently been carrying out some remarkable experiments in telepathy, with his daughter Mrs Arnold Toynbee acting as the agent. I knew nothing of these experiments, but Leslie was buzzing with them.

So there we were, the two of us, waiting for him in my shabby rooms with his manuscript on the table and next to it the manuscript of the two poems that John Masefield had sent us. As the story centres round one of these poems, which was called 'On Growing Old', I will quote part of it.

Be with me, Beauty, for the fire is dying,
My dog and I are old, too old for roving;
Man, whose young passion sets the spindrift flying,
Is soon too lame to march, too cold for loving.
I take the book and gather to the fire,
Turning old yellow leaves. Minute by minute
The clock ticks to my heart; a withered wire
Moves a thin ghost of music in the spinet.

We were both in a state of some elation, filled with a sense that the world was at our feet and that we were playing a vital part in the destiny of nations. Here I must break a rule, and invent dialogue to speed up the story. But 'invent' is really too harsh a word; there are some conversations that echo down the years; and though the tones and tempos may vary, the substance remains.

SELF. Do you want him to go into a trance?

HORE-BELISHA. He doesn't go into trances. He goes out of the room, and when he's outside, somebody thinks of some scene or some incident, very intensely. As a rule his daughter acts as the agent. Then he comes back, holds her hand, and describes what's been in her mind.

SELF. If you think that I'm going to sit here in semi-darkness holding hands with the Regius Professor of Greek you're very much mistaken. If anybody came in we'd both be sent down.

HORE-BELISHA. You don't *have* to hold hands.

SELF. Apart from that we can't possibly ask him to go out and sit on the staircase. He'd catch his death.

HORE-BELISHA. He doesn't have to go out. We can think of something beforehand.

SELF. Such as?

HORE-BELISHA (who had evidently worked this out in advance). Such as the Masefield poems. He knows Masefield personally. They live practically next door to one another. The poems are very much in our minds. And they've got a very definite subject. Old age. With a lot of images. Dogs, fires, clocks, etc. I know the first one by heart.

SELF. So do I.

HORE-BELISHA. Well . . . there you are.

Here ends the invented dialogue, though 'invented', as I said before, is too harsh a term. The bit about holding hands has, I fear, an authentic echo.

Murray arrived on the dot of ten. He was all charm and gentle sympathy. He treated us, not as undergraduates, but as fellow-workers in a great cause, and he patiently submitted to our criticisms of his article, which is very well worth reading as a period piece, even today.

Then came the great moment. Leslie, who had the cunning of the serpent—as the House of Commons was later to discover—brought up the subject of telepathy. Before the Professor had time to draw breath he was somehow relating telepathy with the League of Nations. Here I will not attempt to invent dialogue because I could not hope to recapture Leslie's verbal dexterity, but the general idea was that 'if all men could read each other's minds' . . . 'if the leaders of the nations could achieve a spiritual harmony that transcended the printed word . . .' etc., etc.

Murray fell for it. He warned us that nothing would probably happen but he was quite willing to humour us. Within a few moments the Masefield manuscript was in his hands. It was folded up and he could not possibly have known by whom it was written nor what it was about.

Silence. The two of us sat there staring at him, going over the poem in our minds. Murray closed his eyes. The picture is very clear before me. The scholarly face, the kindly lines about the mouth, the thin folded hands, all lit by the ethereal glow of a fading fire. Then he said—and this is one sentence I can put 'sic' against, for I can still hear it:

'This is all very antique.'

The rest must be impressionistic. But after 'This is all very antique' he definitely mentioned:

1. A dog
2. A fire
3. A clock ticking

And then he said something about music, but added that the music was very faint. And then he got up to go, without even asking us whether he had been on the mark.

Thirty years were to pass before this story clicked into the context of this book, when I was turning over a volume of the Proceedings of the Society for Psychical Research* in which there is an impressive record of the Professor's achievements in this field. There were two series of experiments. In the first, conducted between 1910 and 1915, there were 505 experiments, of which 33 per cent were judged successful. There was then a year's pause. The second series —which coincided with our own experience—lasted from 1916 to 1924, and comprised 36 per cent successes, 23 per cent partial successes and 41 per cent failures.

The procedure was as described in our fragment of 'invented' dialogue, with Murray going out of the room while the agent 'held' a thought, and then returning and usually grasping the agent's hand. At a later date he wrote an account of the atmosphere in which conditions were most favourable for success:

Any disturbance of our customary method, change of time or place, presence of strangers, controversy and especially *noise,* is apt to make things go wrong. When I am getting at the thing which I wish to discover, the only effort I make is a sort of effort of attention of a quite general kind. The thing may come through practically any sense channel, or it may discover a road of its own, a chain of reasoning or of association.

These conditions, admittedly, were not fulfilled in our own case. He was in unfamiliar surroundings and in the presence of strangers. On the other hand, there was silence and there was certainly no 'controversy'. There was a deep sympathy between us because, in spite of the difference of age, we were all intensely animated by the same ideal—a spiritual ideal—the League of Nations. And Hore-Belisha and I both had the poem, with its vivid images, by heart. Indeed, to this day, I could recite it 'in my sleep'.

For those who still doubt the exceptional gifts of this great scholar, who was the last person who would ever have lent his name to any sort of fraudulent practice, the

* Proc. S.P.R., Vol. 29, p. 46; Vol. 34, p. 22.

three following brief examples of his experiments, as recorded in the Proceedings of S.P.R., may bring conviction. They are no more and no less remarkable than hundreds of others which he conducted at Oxford over the years. I have chosen these particular cases because they all occurred in the space of a single evening—an evening in which the professor, obviously, was very much on the ball. The subjects were Rupert Brooke, Napoleon and Rip Van Winkle.

MRS TOYNBEE (*as agent*). I'll think of Ruper [Brooke] meeting Natasha in *War and Peace*. Running in a yellow dress—running through a wood.

PROFESSOR MURRAY. Well, I thought when I came into the room it was about Rupert. Yes, it's fantastic. He's meeting somebody out of a book. He's meeting Natasha in *War and Peace*. I don't know what he is saying—perhaps 'Will you run away with me?'

MRS TOYNBEE. Can't you get the scene?

PROFESSOR MURRAY. I should say it was in a wood.

MRS TOYNBEE. Colour of the dress?

PROFESSOR MURRAY. No, I can't get it.

MISS AGNES MURRAY (*as agent*). Terence [a nephew of Professor Murray] and Napoleon standing on a hill above the Marne and watching the artillery down below.

PROFESSOR MURRAY. This is a war scene—I don't get the persons clearly, but I think on the hill looking down on the artillery. It is not Saumarez. They may be Oxford people. I get the bursting of shells. I should think it was Terence and somebody else—I don't think I know the other person. I don't think I know him.

MR ARNOLD TOYNBEE (*as agent*). I'll do Rip Van Winkle coming down the mountain.

PROFESSOR MURRAY. Oh, I've got this. It's an old sort of gnome-like person with a matted beard coming down— very funny feeling expecting to be known and find things— Oh, it's Rip Van Winkle.

But what does it all *mean*?

Over the centuries a great body of earnest men and women, of varying temperaments, creeds and convictions, have been endeavouring to answer this question, with no very noticeable degree of success. It is therefore hardly likely that I shall be able to answer it. However, one can at least try to clear a little of the ground, by reminding the reader what it does *not* mean.

If one initiates an argument about telepathy at a dinner party one may be quite certain that two things will happen.

Firstly, *everybody* present will have had a telepathic experience which he or she will wish to narrate, usually at inordinate length. There are absolutely no exceptions to this rule. From one's hostess downwards, all along the line, everybody will have something to say. Even the butler—should so distinguished a person be in attendance—will be biting his lips and calling upon all his reserves of self-control, in order to refrain from setting down the soufflé on the sideboard and riveting the company with an account of the peculiar thought-message he had from the cook when she was on holiday and fell off the pier at Bognor Regis.

Not many things are certain in life, but this is one of them.

Secondly, before the discussion has been under way for five minutes, the air will be ringing with two words—'vibrations' and 'radiations'. These two words are, as it were, taken for granted. They are such comforting words, so vivid, and carrying with them so intriguing an undertone of romance! For it is not such a very long step from vibrations and radiations to flutterings of eyelashes and palpitations of hearts.

At this point the habitual diner-out, if he is reading these pages with attention, may perhaps feel a momentary debt of gratitude to the author. For when a suitable moment arrives he will be able to lean forward and observe, with studied nonchalance, that telepathy has nothing whatever to do with 'vibrations' or 'radiations' and that everybody is talking a lot of nonsense. And if he will read on, he will be able to tell them why.

Which means, I fear, that we must get back to work.

15. ECHOES IN THE DARK

At this point we are, then, it seems, faced with the need of another order of energy, not radiant.

PROFESSOR J. B. RHINE

In the last chapter we suggested that the habitual diner-out, if he should find himself involved in any of those controversies about telepathy which are currently so fashionable, may perhaps be grateful to the author of these pages, in which certain common fallacies about this phenomenon are exposed. Of these fallacies the most popular is that which imagines telepathy and clairvoyance to consist in some form of 'radiation' or 'vibration'.

Does this mean that all our spade-work in the previous chapters has been useless—or worse than useless? Were we ourselves contributing to the fallacy when we wrote of the power that 'radiated' from Mesmer's fingers, and when we marvelled at the 'vibrations' dancing from the petals of a daffodil? Are the very words 'vibrations' and 'radiations' fallacious in themselves, and should they be struck out of the vocabulary of the serious investigator?

I hope and believe not. For though we have now reached a point where we shall be obliged to admit the limitations of the radionic theory, this is no reason for tearing up the evidence of the previous chapters. If we take water-divining as the first and most easily comprehensible step in this long and twisting staircase to the stars, we find that these 'radiations' and 'vibrations', of varying potency, *do* exist, *in their own right*.

Let us make this point clearer by a brief 'recap'. The most startling example we have so far encountered of the X Force at work, independent of any human co-operation, was afforded by Professor Maby's investigation of Accident Black Spots. Here we had evidence of the power of a hidden stream to 'tug' the arm of—say—a tired lorry driver, with results which may or may not have been disastrous. Obvi-

148

ously, in such cases, the element of any human co-operation, or indeed, awareness, does not arise. It must have been a case of an independent 'radiation'. The lorry driver was not in a state of trance. He was not driving through the night with dewy eyes and parted lips, listening to the whispers of the fairies. He was doing a job, smoking a fag, and wondering what the wife had for dinner. And then there came this tug.

Take a step further, and see how the physical and psychic territories begin to overlap. Maby himself is 'dowsing'. He is assisted by various scientific devices at which we have glanced, and the whole process, for the moment, is of the earth, earthy. Suddenly, on to the stage, which in this case is the other end of the lawn, steps a woman in a state of emotional tension. She 'bumps the ether', and the hazel twig or the whale-bone, as the case may be, falters in his hand, and the whole experiment goes awry. It is as though a poltergeist had fluttered through the window of his laboratory in order to muddle up his papers and play havoc with his findings.

It is the same all the way down the line. The scientist who endeavours to bring all these phenomena down to earth, to give them, as it were, an aura of respectability, an academic status, is constantly compelled to admit the existence of an element that refuses to be scientifically catalogued. He is like a mathematician whose sums will not come right without the postulation of the symbol X. On the other hand, the psychic who tries to interpret these same phenomena in terms of pure spirit, is equally forcibly reminded—or should be—that the power that 'radiates' from the hands of a man like Michael Ash can be *in itself* as powerful, without the co-operation of the person to whom it is directed, as any mechanical device employed by the pundits of Harley Street.

However, we must now say goodbye, at least for the moment, to 'radiation'.

Professor J. B. Rhine, author of the statement quoted at the outset of this chapter, to the effect that in telepathy we are faced with the need of an order of energy 'not radiant', is probably the world's greatest authority on the subject. For over thirty years, at Duke University, U.S.A., Rhine and his collaborators have been carrying out researches in clairvoyance and telepathy; no other body of investigators in the world has ever covered so wide a range nor examined the manifold aspects of the subject with such tireless tenacity. The very phrase 'Extra-Sensory Perception' * is of Rhine's coining. Though it might not be true to say that what he does not know about it is not worth knowing, he almost certainly knows more about it than anybody else.

Of the thousands of experiments which he has been conducting to prove the 'truth' of telepathy the most impressive, from the point of view of the average man—maybe because he finds them the easiest to understand—have been concerned with card-reading. By 'card-reading' we do not imply anything so banal as 'fortune-telling'; in the Rhine experiments cards were most frequently used merely because they were convenient symbols, of which clear images could be formed in the brain and—for this reason—transmitted from one brain to another.

The five cards most commonly used by Rhine, and by most other investigators, depict a cross, a star, a circle, a square, and a triple band of wavy lines. I myself should have thought that the symbol of the cross, and to a minor extent of the star, would have carried such powerful emotional associations that it would have confused the issue and blurred the vision. However, this is apparently not the case.

Rhine observes:

> The radiation theory is an old one and has been frequently discussed in connection with telepathy. Even the mediumistic jargon often includes 'getting into the vibration'. Brain 'waves' were supposed to be emitted by the agent and intercepted by the brain of the percipient.

However, he points out that in order to cover the telepathic phenomena the 'wave' theory would demand that

---

* J. B. Rhine, PH.D., *Extra-Sensory Perception* (Faber & Faber, 1935). See also *The Reach of the Mind* (Faber & Faber, 1948).

  Some purists have objected to the term E.S.P. on the ground that the phenomena may not be 'perception' at all, since the percipient of telepathic information can never know when his interpretation is right or wrong. For this reason they have substituted the twenty-third letter of the Greek alphabet, *psi*, as a sort of 'blanket' term for all psychic matters, including clairvoyance, telepathy and 'pre-recognition'. I prefer the commoner title E.S.P. because it is a convenient portmanteau for a number of problems which, though divergent in their expression, appear to be essentially similar in their nature and their source.

there would have to be rays originating not only in the agent's brain but *in the cards themselves.*

He continues:

> Now, the cardboard is slightly opaque to X-rays but the ink-figures on it are not. An X-ray photograph of the card shows only a dim outline after a ten-second exposure. There is no difference made by the figures printed on the cards—no differential absorption. If these rays are not obstructed by the ink-figures it is surely not to be expected that shorter ones would be. And if longer waves were in question, the cardboard would interfere. And even if these difficulties were not in the way, even if there were a suitable ray penetrating the pack of cards, *giving differential absorption on every card,* the impression given on a receptive plate or organ would be one big blur in the centre of the card.

After some more highly technical argument he sums it up by saying: 'Suppose one were trying to distinguish visually 25 luminous figures set one behind the other, when he was seated from 2—5 feet away from them, the result would be one great unanalysable splodge.'

Moreover, in telepathic work, the card-pack may be perceived *from any angle,* but on the ray assumption the angle would be as important as it is to a photographer.

Another seemingly insurmountable obstacle to the acceptance of the ray theory is posed by the whole problem of distance. 'All radiant energy declines in intensity with the square of the distance from the source.' We should therefore expect to find that, other things being equal, distance would bring about a sharp decline in the accuracy of the results obtained by the card-method of testing telepathy. But precisely the opposite is the case: 'distance telepathy' has actually proved to be *more* accurate than telepathy in the same room.

Here we may pause to note the immense amount of research that lies behind this brief observation. No less than 3,300 trials were made 'in the same room' and 2,100 'at some distance'. Throughout these trials the accuracy of the result was noticeably in favour of the 'distance' test, at times sensationally so. The most remarkable example quoted by Rhine in this connection is afforded by a certain Miss Turner. Using packs of 25 cards her 'close-up' average was 7.7. But when the distance was extended to 250 miles her

average was 19. Nineteen cards right out of twenty-five—
seventy-six out of a hundred, again and again! Facts like
these, facts which can be verified to the last syllable before
the most sceptical jury, are surely of more lasting interest
than most of the things one reads in the newspapers, particularly when one realizes that behind the facts lies another fact
that is, as it were, 'faceless' . . . for Rhine's summing-up
is that 'any radiation hypothesis depending on the inverse
square law can hardly be regarded as plausible, in my judgment. And if it be a radiation hypothesis without the inverse square law, what would it be?'

Not for the first time we seem to be asking questions that
cannot be answered.

To suggest that Professor Rhine is a tragic figure on the
American stage would be misleading; by every standard of
personal and public achievement he is entitled to regard his
life as a success, and let us hope that many years of exciting
exploration be ahead of him.

And yet, if we read his formidable body of work with an
ear for the personal undertones we catch an echo of frustration and loneliness. Boldly he called one of his later books
New World of the Mind,* and when he was a young man,
and first sailed out to explore these dark uncharted seas, it
was with a stout heart and a high hope that one day he
would come home to port with a detailed map of that 'new
world' in his luggage. He has not done so, and the fact that
nobody else has done so is no great consolation. When he
confesses this in his foreword you can almost hear the sigh
in the writing:

New worlds, of course, are not discovered all at once.
A new hemisphere may be glimpsed first only as a few
small islands, or an electric universe as a few tiny sparks.

And then he adds, drily, that 'this task of completion is
commonly a long one.'

What's more, each time that he does come home to port,
bearing with him the rough sketch of another little island,
or revealing soundings of waters deeper than any hitherto
known to man, he finds, when he displays his data in the
form of a book, not exactly a lack of public attention, but a
strange shifting of interest, as though the average man was
unable to understand what was really important about them.

* Faber & Faber, 1954.

Consider the whole question of psi and the light it throws, or fails to throw, on the eternal—and one would have thought vital—problem of personal survival after death. With my incorrigible habit of putting things into headlines, I suggest that if Professor Rhine had been a journalist he might have found himself scribbling such phrases as the following at the top of his copy:

> DEATH BORES AMERICA
> SURVIVAL PROBLEM GETS A BIG YAWN
> HEAVEN AND HELL ON THE WAY OUT

There is no need to apologize for this vulgarity; there is nothing wrong about a headline if it makes us think and if it crystallizes the content of the message that follows it. And this is precisely the message—to me a very melancholy message—inherent in the sober passages in which the Professor discusses the problem which, until the last few decades, has towered above all other questions which man has asked since the world began . . . do we survive death? After observing that the whole range and nature of psi research is far more complicated than had been realized at the outset, and seems likely to become even more so, he states:

> But it is an equally serious fact that while the difficulties of the investigation have grown greater, *public interest in the survival problem as a research objective has grown almost proportionately smaller.*

If we read that sentence again, and if we realize that every word of Rhine's is weighed in the balance, and checked and counter-checked by a formidable array of facts, we may perhaps feel that the headlines were not so uncalled for.

So where do we stand, if we are among the apparently diminishing number who still regard the question as important? What answer do we get to the great question mark—using all the data of the psi investigators, particularly their researches into mediumship, to help us? Let the Professor tell us:

'The outcome is best described as a draw.'

It is a somewhat dusty answer.

But it is when we come to this great American's conclusions on the significance of his life's work, to date, that the temptation to use headlines becomes irresistible. Not long ago I wrote a letter to him. I have not the letter by me, but the theme of it might be contained in a question of six words: 'Has it all been worth while?' All the painstaking research, year after year, all the card-shuffling, all the meticulous analysis, all the peering into the shadows? He replied to the letter, with his usual courtesy, but he did not really reply to the questions . . . not because they are unanswerable but because he has already answered them in the body of his work. And the answer is that it has not only been worth while but that it has been of paramount importance, not only in itself, as a fascinating by-path of science but *as a force with the potential to save the world from destruction.*

And this is where our headlines come in again:

STAGGERING CLAIMS BY AMERICAN SCIENTIST
THE CRYSTAL MIGHTIER THAN THE ATOM?
FIGHTING THE REDS WITH A PACK OF CARDS

Are we justified in concocting these sensational slogans from the findings of Duke University? Most certainly. If words mean anything at all, the message of the headlines is implicit in such passages as this:

In the present world struggle of ideologies the West cannot afford to let its people remain half physicalistic and half idealistic (that is, spiritualistic) in their philosophy. The moral force of a country can well be the deciding factor in a struggle, and that force depends upon how sure its people are of the rightness of their stand. In terms of effectiveness over cost, unified group attitude is probably the best kind of armament there is. Plainly, then, Western leadership needs to get to the bottom of its intellectual issues with communism. If the communist ideology is phony, then clearly the facts that show it to be so ought to be revealed, reinforced, and exploited to the full. *Nothing, however, but the authority of science at its best could carry world conviction—and hold it— on such a point.*

After asking whether enough people of the right sort can be brought to see this 'causal dimension of communism' before it is too late, he goes on to ask the 64,000-dollar question:

The whole ethical integrity of the world is at stake in the moral challenge of communism. If communism is not a new and distinctive way of treating fellowmen in the mass, what *is* it? The first and great question about it then should be: Does it have a sound premise of incontestable facts? *All the evidence from parapsychology flatly contradicts this. What is more, parapsychology is the ONLY science that does so in a rigorous and unequivocal fashion.*

And what is the inevitable conclusion from these facts? How do we put to practical use the 'flat contradictions' of parapsychology? (Which have emerged, remember, from all those painful experiments with such things as cards and crystals.) By research and yet more research, on an international scale, into the *non-physical aspects of men.* Such a programme of research, says Rhine, could become 'a new unifying influence in Western life, a central factor of understanding. It could unite our own house that is divided, our own hearts that are not whole, towards this root issue of materialism of which communism is the bitter, prickly fruit.'

How about those headlines now? Are not these, in very truth, 'staggering claims'? And yet, why should they be so staggering? If the work of the psi investigators could arrive at a stage where the non-physical aspects of man could be made so apparent that no scientist of whatever political colour could afford to ignore them, is it not blindingly obvious that the very foundations of the communist creed would crumble over-night? A single miracle of Christ would put the whole communist world in turmoil. Indeed, any 'miracle' —using the word in its most pedestrian sense to indicate the subservience of matter to some over-ruling spiritual power— *any* miracle, scientifically attested, makes nonsense of the whole communist ideology. These miracles are happening every day, all over the world. Bodies are being healed without the material aid of drugs, brains are communicating without the material aid of mechanical devices, and though the validity of communications from the world after death is not yet scientifically established beyond a degree of fifty per cent —'the outcome', said Professor Rhine, 'is best described as a draw'—a fifty per cent 'margin of error' would be a great deal too much for the dedicated Marxist to accept. Even a one per cent margin would cause him a great deal of soul-searching, if he had a soul to search. Communism cannot grant a millionth of a percentage of error in its materialistic creed. It dare not admit even a farthing's worth of light. For communism slams the door that leads to an after-life, and stamps on the grave of all immortal aspirations.

If the leaders of the communist world were really far-sighted, their Number One target, in the ultimate struggle that may await us, would not be the launching-sites of the rockets, nor the secret tunnels in which the West is guarding its poisons and its gold. They would choose a target which held a far greater ultimate menace to their hopes of world domination. They would aim at a far more important address.

The address would be Duke University, Durham, North Carolina, U.S.A.

And I believe that the Communists, in their blundering monolithic way, are dimly aware of the threat which may be awaiting them in those quiet laboratories of the mind. For I have had personal experience of their almost pathological hatred of spiritualism, and the violence with which they react against any author who supports—or even refrains from attacking—the evidence of parapsychology, or indeed of any spiritual interpretation of man's being.

Some years ago I was commissioned by a London newspaper to write a survey of the world's great religions. One day, during the course of these inquiries, I found myself wandering past the offices of the *Daily Worker*, and on the spur of the moment I walked in and sent up my card with a request to see the editor. I thought that it might be interesting to find out if there were still any people who called themselves 'Christian Communists'. (There *have* been such oddities, even though the phrase is of necessity quite meaningless.) The editor was out but I made contact with an amiable little man, presumably one of the staff and certainly one of the faithful, who said he would be glad to answer my questions. The dialogue, which took place against the usual background of portraits of Marx and Lenin, was pretty flat at the beginning and at this distance of time I will not attempt to reproduce it; my questions were probably uninspired and the answers were certainly unilluminating—they were all based on the familiar theme of 'complete religious freedom' in Russia. I was even shown a fly-blown photograph of a lot of people queueing outside a cathedral in Moscow.

I was about to get up and leave, with apologies for wasting

RADIO CAB

227-1212

DUAL CHANNEL DISPATCHING
FOR FASTER SERVICE

131 +2   7
133 +5   8
138   9
143 +1   12
144 +1   1
145 +2   2
147 +1   3
148 +2   4
150 +7   5
151 +3
153

his time, when at random I asked a question about spiritualism and the whole subject of 'psi' research. After all, some of the greatest mediums in the world had come from Russia. As for the scientific aspect of it, was it not possible that there might be a sort of 'psychic Pavlov', endeavouring to make experiments on the souls of dogs? I was not trying to lay a trap, I was genuinely interested.

Immediately, sparks began to fly. The reaction was quite extraordinary; it was as though the poor man had been personally insulted. Springing to his feet he declared that there were no mediums in Russia. Such creatures were regarded as parasites. They were in the same class as 'gypsies' —this rather odd word comes back clearly over the years— they had no social status. Nor were there any crystal gazers nor 'card-sharpers'—another word that has stuck. As for such 'capitalist' institutions as the Society for Psychical Research! And here he could scarcely bring himself to speak. From the vehemence with which he attacked the poor Society you would think that it was some stronghold of capitalism employing battalions of enslaved poltergeists to snatch the crusts from the lips of the deserving poor.

This went on for quite a while. It was very interesting. My reporter's nose told me that I was 'on' to something. And then, like a fool, I asked a question that was too much for him.

'You mean', I said, 'that if Karl Marx had been confronted with a single scientifically attested case of telepathy —just one—he would have felt unable to write *Das Kapital?*'

That finished it. He made no attempt to reply to the question. It was altogether too outrageous. Without another word he walked to the door and flung it open. As it slammed behind me, and as I walked down the staircase, I thought again: 'Yes, there is a story here.' But I never wrote it. For it was not till I had learned of the work of Professor Rhine, and his own interpretation of it in the light of the world crisis, that I was to understand its full significance.

Is there any chance that the Western world at large will ever realize the immense forces that are at its disposal in the researches of Duke University—forces more potentially explosive than all the uranium in the world? The prospects are not too hopeful. One of the hindrances to the general acceptance of an idea so novel, and indeed so bizarre, is the fact that the average man, who is not conscious of any special psychic gifts, and who has had no psychic experiences, may assume that for this reason it is 'none of his business'. Surely this is a rather unenterprising attitude? The results of the Rhine investigations are not cloaked in mystery; they are open to inspection by the whole world. Again, the philosophy of the communist powers is not whispered in secret; it is shouted from the housetops day in and day out. Given the facts, and given the philosophy, does it need any exceptional powers of reasoning, let alone of psychic awareness, to realize that the one cancels out the other? After all, that is all that I have been trying to do in the foregoing pages. I was not writing with the aid of a crystal ball; none of the conclusions I have been drawing have been dependent on any personal psychic pretensions.

And here, perhaps, I may be forgiven for adding yet another 'personal note'. Once or twice in this book—if not more often—I may have irritated the reader by appearing to lay claim to some special 'sensibility' in psychic matters. This is a common human weakness, maybe more prevalent in women than in men. If you wish to put a woman in a good humour the best way of doing so, apart from remarking that she is wearing the prettiest hat you ever saw, is to assure her that she 'must be psychic'. This invariably produces the purrs.

I have a dim feeling that from time to time I may have assumed this irritating posture of 'extra awareness', as when I boasted that I had the gift of water-divining. Perhaps I should not have made this boast, for it is a gift that has manifested itself very seldom and seems, of late, to have dried up altogether.

This may therefore be a fitting moment to confess that as far as telepathy is concerned—with two possible exceptions to which we will later refer—I am a total flop.

For hours on end I have sat with intimate friends on opposite sides of a table going through packs of cards, trying to guess whether they were black or red, with results as totally ignominious as my efforts to guess whether the things on the Stock Exchange were going up or down. Whenever I decided to be black the cards went red, in precisely the same way as whenever I decided to be bull the market went bear.

Anyway, in telepathic matters, I must be the world's low. I have tied myself into knots trying to get 'in touch', wandered about the smooth-shaven lawn, gazed at the inconstant moon, clenched my fists, purged my mind, or tried to purge it, of all distracting influences, in order to convey to the 'percipient'—whoever he or she might be—that I was possessed by the soul of Chopin, and at that very moment engaged in writing the simple melodic line of the Berceuse. I could see that melodic line in my mind as clearly as the graph on a weather chart, I could respond—I *was* responding—to its exquisite influences. I was saturated with the thing, singing with it, I *was* that piece of music. But what happened, when I staggered back exhausted to the figure in the deck-chair, sitting under the walnut tree? She invariably said something like: 'Was it anything to do with fish?'

After this humiliating confession I may perhaps be forgiven for recounting a personal experience of so strange a nature that it is difficult to explain without assuming that some sort of telepathic influence was involved. Even this experience I should have been inclined to keep to myself were it not capable of being verified, not by the testimony of friends but by the impartial witness of recorded sound—which is a cumbersome way of describing a tape-recorder. Since such cases must be comparatively rare, this one seems worthy of putting on record.

One morning in October 1963, I was rung up by the Canadian Broadcasting Company, asking if I would be willing to broadcast to Canada on the theme of 'The Cost of British Royalty'. I said that I would be happy to do so, on two conditions. The first was that I should be allowed to develop the theme that the cost of British royalty, to the taxpayer, was ludicrously small. For a few pennies a year he got the most spectacular show on earth. He also got something of greater importance—a code of conduct inspired by Christian principles. He might ignore the example and he might conduct himself with small regard to the code, but they were always there in the background, and in my opinion they gave to the whole of society a quality which we would otherwise have lacked.

'Very well,' they said, 'if that's how you feel about it. And the other condition?'

This was simply that the whole thing should be off the cuff. No script of any sort, not even a 'lead-in' or an exit line. 'Let's just talk and see what happens.'

This is what happened.

We sat on a sofa in a quiet room, and after a brief sound-test our conversation began. I noted the time because the interview had to last fifteen minutes and I wanted to allow enough time to develop the various themes I had in mind. The intention was to sum these up, in the last five minutes, by a picture of the Queen driving down the Mall in her golden coach flanked by an escort of Horse Guards in their flamboyant uniforms, and then—having noted that this was probably regarded by foreigners as an example of royal extravagance—to point out that it was, in fact, nothing of the sort, that it cost the taxpayer not a cent. The coach had been paid for two centuries ago; as for the Horse Guards, they were very far from being chocolate soldiers; they were on the Army Establishment, and though they might be decorative they were fighting men who had served their country with great gallantry in the past and would doubtless do so again in the future.

I glanced at my watch. Five minutes to go. Time to start on this theme. It developed itself very easily and the mental picture was exceptionally vivid; I seemed to see the sunlight sparkling on the polished breastplates and hear the clatter of the horses' hooves . . . that most evocative of all the sounds of London.

Then, without any warning, I had a sharp feeling of discomfort, almost of nausea, accompanied by an acute headache. The picture of the Queen and her cavalcade vanished as swiftly as if it had been blacked out in a theatrical performance, to be replaced by an equally vivid picture of President Kennedy driving in an open car, flanked by his escort of motor-bicyclists with their snarling exhausts. And, as though it were being dictated to me, I began to describe this scene.

All this, I repeat, is on the tape—apart, of course, from the feeling of nausea and headache, to which there can be no witness but myself. But everything else is there: the crowd, the cavalcade of cops, and my faintly derogatory remarks about the security precautions which were apparently necessary in a great democracy as opposed to the minimum of fuss with which the Queen moved among her people. Speaking very quickly, I followed the procession down the street until it vanished round the corner. Then back to England with a few phrases of rounding off and the interview was over.

The interviewer held up his hand and flicked his fingers. He switched off the recorder.

'O.K. That was swell. Fifteen minutes to the dot.'

I felt rather pleased with myself. Evidently, he hadn't noticed the emotional tension of the last few minutes. I said: 'Wasn't the ending a bit abrupt?'

'Sure. But that's how we like it.' He pressed a button and the tape spun back. 'Let's play back the last part. Your switch to Kennedy took me off my guard. But it was a good curtain.'

He pressed another button. Back came my voice. The last phrases about the Queen. The switch to Kennedy, in a different tempo. Then his own voice: 'Thank you, Mr Nichols, etc. etc.'

He turned off the machine. I sat back and lit a cigarette.

'Let's do another, one of these days,' said the interviewer, rising from the sofa.

'I'd like to.'

'And now, I think we've earned a drink.'

He walked to the door and opened it. I followed him. As we stepped outside we heard the sound of footsteps running. A little man with a white face turned the corner. He came to a halt in front of us. He stared at us, not quite seeing us.

'President Kennedy', he blurted out, 'has been assasinated. Six minutes ago.'

We stayed there, for a second or two, looking at each other like waxworks. Then the little man ran away.

We walked down the corridor, saying little. We had our drink. My friend did not refer to the 'coincidence' of the broadcast in connection with the assassination; there was no reason why he should do so because for him it *was* merely a 'coincidence'; he had no knowledge of my personal feelings during the interview. But for me, in retrospect, it seems like something that might be described as 'a moment of truth'.

If I were 'polishing up' this story to make it a perfect example of telepathy, I should be tempted to persuade myself that I had visualized the President against the actual Dallas setting where the tragedy occurred. I didn't. I saw him very clearly in quite a different setting—at the Park Avenue end of East Seventy Second in New York City. When I had been in America during the previous winter I had often stood at the window of an apartment on the ninth floor of 765 E. 72nd watching him as he drove down after one of his luncheons at the Carlyle Hotel. And I had often thought how easy it would be for some little madman to look down on him, and raise his rifle, and fire a shot that would echo round the world. So maybe it was just a 'coincidence'. All I can say, in the vernacular, is that it shook *me*.

But if it was not coincidence, what was it?

We might perhaps find a clue to this in the 'group-mind' conception which has recently been engaging the attention of a number of eminent biologists.

Translated from the animal to the human kingdom, the 'group-mind' would assume a sort of pool of common consciousness, or rather sub-consciousness, across which the varied fleets of humanity were sailing. If we postulate such a pool, we might also admit the idea that some of the ripples on its surface caused by those disturbers of the peace who are throwing in their pebbles from the banks, might evoke a specially sharp reaction from a few persons who were exceptionally sensitive psychic sailors. And at the risk of entangling ourselves too deeply in this metaphor, that a specially large pebble hurled with unusual violence into the centre of the pool—such as the bullet which killed the President—might evoke an exceptionally violent response. However, such an assumption would oblige us to expect that a very large number of persons all over the world had also experienced emotions similar to my own at the moment of the President's death. If they did, they kept very quiet about it.

All the same, I am inclined to believe that there is 'something in' the concept of the 'group-mind'. For if we are prepared, as we must be, to credit the humblest forms of insect life with this miraculous gift of 'mass communication', does it not seem absurd, to say the least of it, that we should deny this same gift to man? Natural history abounds in examples of a 'group-mind' exercising its mysterious control over communities of such insects as ants and bees. The flight of birds through the air, of minnows through the water, seems to be modified not merely by such measurable influences as the force of wind or the degree of temperature or even the drive of hunger, but by something else, something invisible, something silent, and yet—to them—as clearly seen and heard as though they were members of an orchestra obeying the dictates of a conductor's baton. The biologist might reply that this 'group instinct' is not such as should command the special respect of man, let alone his envy—any more than a man should envy a dog for the sensitivity of its nose or a cat for the mobility of its ears. 'We have risen above all that sort of thing,' he might say.

But have we? Do we even wish to do so? Has not the conception of a 'group-mind' a certain innate nobility? To argue that it is in some way despicable merely because it is a gift enjoyed by the animal kingdom is a piece of sheer human insolence. There are many fields of activity in which the animal kingdom could give salutary lessons to the kingdoms of mankind. One of them is the battlefield. If we were to ask the animals to wage war on our 'superior' human level, we should be obliged—say—to require all the black cats in Sussex to rush over the border in order to scratch out the eyes of all the tabbies in Surrey, and to go on doing so until one or the other was exterminated, and the rats reigned supreme in a desolated land.

A long way from President Kennedy? Not really, for the 'group-mind' is the only explanation which seems to make sense of my little broadcasting story. To some people, no doubt, the theory will seem faintly ridiculous, to others it will seem not only sane but inevitable, even though they cannot explain it. I shall always remember, as a very young man, reading a certain passage in the mystical experiences of the Reverend Vale Owen, which were published in a paper on which I was then a reporter, the *Sunday Dispatch*. The series, as a whole, might be described as a sort of personally conducted tour of heaven, though that would perhaps give a wrong impression. Vale Owen was no vulgarian; he was passionately sincere and almost frighteningly ascetic; and he wrote extremely well. Moreover, he refused to accept a penny piece for his efforts; he only wanted to tell the truth as it had been revealed to him.

The particular passage which so moved me concerned a strange vision of a flock of birds. I cannot recall in which of the courts of heaven it came to him, but I can see those birds to this day, preening themselves on the marble pavements, like the pigeons in Venice, gathering closer and closer to one another, and then—merging into *one* bird, a bird of the greatest beauty. And though I read this in somewhat unsympathetic circumstances, sitting in the news-room at midnight, surrounded by the journalistic uproar of typewriters and telephones, I said to myself: 'But of course, this is the most natural thing that could ever be; this is what birds *must* do, this is when they fly out of this world to wherever their wings may take them. They *must* blend together into a sort of super Bird, their songs *must* harmonize into one song, more exquisite than the song of any nightingale, singing in the woods alone.'

16. THE SLUMBERING CHURCH

The 'why' is plain as way to parish Church.
                      SHAKESPEARE: *As You Like It*

The Little Church of St Peter's in Petersham is one of the prettiest in the county of Surrey. You reach it by a narrow lane that turns off the main road to Richmond and after a few paces you are in the heart of the country. Or you can approach it by another lane that runs from the River Thames, flanked by water-meadows, with a distant view of Richmond Hill. Walking up this lane is one of the pleasantest parts of the whole ceremony of going to church, particularly when there is a gentle breeze from the south, carrying the music of the bells down the meadows. If you are early, you can spend a tranquil ten minutes in the old graveyard, which always seems to carry a faint tang of the distant sea, for here a number of gallant sailors lie at rest. Of these the most eminent, as many Canadian visitors will remember, is George Vancouver who died at Petersham in 1798.

Like so many ancient churches in Britain, St Peter's is something of an architectural muddle; the Normans join pious hands with the Tudors, who link with the Georgians, and finally find themselves in the company of the early Victorians. But the main impression is of the eighteenth century, for this is one of the few English churches which have retained the lofty old Georgian pew boxes. So tall are these that ladies of modest proportions, when they take their seats, can scarcely peer over the top, so that if one is sitting at the back one sees only their hats, like clumps of flowers dotted round an herbaceous border.

During the writing of this book I have often worshipped at St Peter's, wandered up the little lane, crossed the porch and knelt on the shabby hassock to pray. And then sat back again, hoping against hope that a few more people would trickle in. At the risk of sounding irreverent I have sometimes been reminded of one's feelings in a theatre, when a play is not doing too well, particularly if one is the author of it. One counts the house. Only two minutes to the hour, and there are still only four in the congregation. Suddenly there are footsteps in the porch, and in comes a family of three. One hopes that they will sit under the pulpit, to make a nice show, but they drift rather timidly to a back pew, where they are lost. A pity.

More footsteps. A mother and two children. They sit in a prominent position, which is desirable in some ways, but not in others, for the children are terrible fidgets. Nearly zero hour, and in a moment we shall all be standing up for the entrance of the vicar. Then, a positive scurry of footsteps, and in comes the eccentric woman whose name I have never learned, and two small sulky boy scouts, and a rather puzzled-looking couple in horn-rimmed spectacles—probably Canadians who have been paying a pilgrimage to Vancouver's tomb. Standing on tiptoe, with the assistance of the shabby hassock, one makes a rapid calculation. If we count the eccentric woman—who should not be included, because on alternate Sundays she attends a theosophical 'new-thought' service in West Hampstead—and if we count the boy scouts as 'wholes', though they should really be 'halves', being so very small and so very sulky—we arrive at the glorious total of fifteen.

People's reasons for going to church are many and various. Some—and these are a rapidly diminishing number—go out of habit; some go because they are lonely, some because they are afraid. My own reason, at any rate during the period in which this book was being written, was to try to clear my mind. My head was buzzing with strange noises, and voices speaking in a language that I scarcely understood, and my eyes were tired from gazing at miracles which I could not properly interpret. To say that I wished to submit this blotched and tangled manuscript to the scrutiny of Christ would sound embarrassingly pompous, but that was the rough idea. In church you are—or should be—as close to Christ as you are likely to get; you are—or should be—'illuminated' by the radiance of His astonishing mind, which is not only topical but one step ahead of any of the news with which the world is echoing, and always will be. Was it not possible,

as I knelt on that shabby hassock, that some of this illumination might be granted to me, even if it only served to tell me,
in all this bewilderment, who was on His side? And—maybe
even more important—who was not?

But I drew a blank. There was no illumination. This was
in no way due to any lack of devotion on the part of the
priests, who were dedicated and selfless men of God, and
extremely intelligent men too. Nor to any sense that the little
church was not a temple in which Christ was pleased to enter.
Rather was there a nagging feeling that the Church as a
whole, the Church with a capital C, was largely uninterested
in the problems which were bedevilling me, and indeed almost unaware of them. True, the kindly and learned arch-
deacon who administered the sacrament was not unaware;
indeed, I had sometimes discussed them with him in a desul-
tory fashion. But I wanted the *whole* Church to be tingling
with excitement, even if it was an angry excitement, and
even if minister after minister rose in his pulpit to denounce
men like de la Warr as lackeys of the Devil and the Box as
an instrument of Satan. But there was only the same faint
rustle of prayer-books—fewer and fewer prayer-books—
opening and shutting at the same place.

Here I must make a confession, which puts me in a poor
light as a serious investigator. During the whole of this period
of questioning and frustration I was only dimly aware of the
work of the Churches' Fellowship for Psychical and Spiritual
Studies, and had met none of its distinguished advocates.
How I came to remedy this omission need not concern us,
but after doing so I am happy to acknowledge that there is,
in some branches of the Church, a stirring of interest in
psychic matters. However, the stirring is only faint; by no
stretch of the imagination can it be described as animating
the whole body with a 'tingle of excitement'. For this reason I
shall allow the foregoing passages, with their note of im-
patience and frustration, to stand.

If the British people—or the American people, or any
other people in Christendom—had the smallest sense of the
priorities, they would regard the aims and beliefs of the
Churches' Fellowship for Psychical and Spiritual Studies* as
among the most important in the world. For the Fellowship
believes that the gifts of the Holy Spirit to the Church are

* Founded in 1954. Particulars from 54 Denison House, Vauxhall
Bridge Road, London, SW 1.

meant to be permanent and exercised *today*, and that their gifts should be dedicated to the service of God and of mankind. The operative word, of course, is *today*. We live in an age which some are pleased to regard as an age of Reason—a somewhat ironic appellation for an era in which we frame our policies with the apparent object of enabling us to emulate the example of the Gadarene swine. But if we could be transported through time, and be set down outside Jerusalem, in the light of the coldest and bitterest dawn that ever broke on the world . . . if we could walk through the fields of wild irises, wet with dew, and see in the distance the cross that man had erected as a symbol of his total rejection of his Creator, we should probably be prepared for miracles and I think that we should get them. We should feel very close to the sky, and we should not feel that the sky was untenanted. As we neared the city, and listened to the tales of the travellers on the dusty roads, we should not dismiss them as so much idle gossip. Why should they be so greatly in awe, so greatly uplifted and—sometimes—so greatly afraid? The sceptic's answer, if he could bring himself to make this imaginary journey into the past, might be that any 'feelings of awe' which we experienced would be due to the fact that we should be stepping into an age of credulity, in which little was known about the laws of nature—an age when a miraculous explanation was often given to quite natural phenomena. But surely the fact that men are willing to believe does not necessarily invalidate their beliefs? Is it not at least equally probable that an unwillingness to believe might cause them to reject valid evidence and cloud their interpretation of it? Wishful thinking operates in the direction of scepticism as well as belief.

It was because the Churches' Fellowship accented the word 'today' that I felt so greatly drawn towards it. Here, so it seemed, were men and women who were studying psychic phenomena, and not only reconciling them with their Christian beliefs but claiming that these beliefs were actually strengthened and illuminated by their findings. One of the first expositions of its aims that came my way* contains the following passage:

* Canon J. D. Pearce-Higgins, Vice-Provost of Southwark, *Religion, Science and the Paranormal* published in 1964 by Churches' Fellowship for Psychical and Spiritual Study, 54 Denison House, Vauxhall Bridge Road, London, SW1. 3s. 6d.

We owe a great debt to the Spiritualist movement, as also to Christian Science, for drawing the attention of the orthodox body to its neglect of vital factors in its own tradition, psychic phenomena, and spiritual and mental healing. All religions can learn from each other, and there are probably many things we can learn from Christian Science and Spiritualists. At least it behoves us to remain on terms of good-will and Christian charity with those with whom we share a belief in the value of the human soul, and of its immortality. *We are Christians inside the Christian Church seeking to rediscover the fullness of our own faith.*

When I read that passage I thought of the little church of St Peter's with its tall eighteenth-century pews, most of them empty. I went on thinking, and the picture widened to include a very green and prosperous landscape stretching from Richmond to Kingston, plentifully sprinkled with millionaires. For a moment the picture narrowed again, so that I could see into the minds of those millionaires, which were like so many computing machines, ticking away happily in a golden rhythm. But now and then one of the machines would suddenly stop, and there was an awful silence, because computing machines are not supposed to stop, and the millionaires thought it in very bad taste that anything should stop, particularly as they knew it would stop for ever. A few of the millionaires, indeed, were so disturbed that they glanced uneasily over their shoulders in the direction of the little church, as though they had suddenly remembered that the church did repairs for that sort of thing. However, by now, the computing machines were all ticking away again, the unpleasantness was forgotten, and once more the picture widened. It widened far beyond the aforesaid green and prosperous landscape, it soared up and up into the higher airs, and those airs were full of music and voices. Not always sweet music and not always soothing voices. There were discords and there were warnings. But . . . most emphatically . . . there was not silence.

At this point I sat down, took out my pen, and wrote to Canon Pearce-Higgins, Vice-Provost of Southwark. He is vice-chairman of the Fellowship and one of its most dynamic protagonists. Then I addressed another envelope to Mrs Rosalind Heywood, whom we have met before in her capacity as the author of two brilliant studies in extra-sensory perception—*The Sixth Sense** and *The Infinite Hive*.† Mrs Heywood is not nominally a Christian, but it is difficult to apply to her the somewhat arid description of 'agnostic', as defined in the Oxford Dictionary . . . 'one who holds that the existence of anything beyond material phenomena e.g. of a First Cause, or of noumena, cannot be known.' She is a difficult person to sum up. If I were to attempt to do so in a single Chestertonian phrase I would suggest that, somewhat like Shelley, she believes in marvels but not in miracles. Indeed, she shies at the very word 'miracle'. For the moment we can leave it at that, as she will shortly be speaking for herself.

Both these envelopes contained invitations to dinner, and both invitations were accepted. Here is a record of the conversation which resulted.

Scene. The fireside of the music-room in a country cottage. On a near-by table is a tape-recorder.

Dramatis Personae. Canon John Pearce-Higgins, Mrs Rosalind Heywood and myself.

Time. The present. Shortly after dinner.

B.N. I hope we aren't feeling too self-conscious because of the tape-recorder but it's a necessary evil. I'll begin by saying that I'd like to see the little church of St Peter's full to the brim, and that it might well be full if people, when they went inside, knew that the Church was going to give them some *positive* assurance of life after death—an assurance based not only on the promises contained in Holy Scripture but reinforced by constant and unremitting psychical research.

CANON P.H. So you want to talk about death?

B.N. If you don't mind. Has Mrs Heywood any objection?

MRS H. On the contrary. Considering that—apart from birth—death is the one and only topic of conversation under the sun that we all have in common it has often struck me as faintly ironic that we never seem able to mention it.

CANON P.H. Here of course is the 64,000-dollar question— the question which the Churches' Fellowship came into being to try to answer. I don't think that we're doing it terribly well, though perhaps it isn't altogether our fault. You see, it's frowned upon to discuss the whole matter of

---

* Chatto & Windus, 1959.
† Chatto & Windus, 1964.

death. It's frowned upon socially and it's frowned upon politically. We're told that we've 'never had it so good' and the State doesn't want us to be reminded that there will come a moment when this condition of existence will cease. It's depressing, it's against policy, it's bad form. (To Mrs Heywood) Can you bear with me if I speak for a moment of the history of the Protestant Church?

MRS H. I'm always ready to be instructed in the history of churches.

CANON P.H. The brutal fact is that the Protestant Church, at the time of the Reformation, dropped an iron curtain between the living and the dead. It's an appalling thing to say, if you realize its full implications, but it has to be said. Mind you, the Protestant Church had very good reasons for doing so. There were endless abuses, imported from Rome: masses for the dead, chantry chapels, pilgrimages, spurious relics, the whole shoddy apparatus of superstition, which all had to be paid for. And all over Western Europe people were no longer prepared to go on paying. So they dropped the iron curtain, with a clang. But by doing so they shut themselves out from the wider theatre of world religion, they lost something vital in the whole drama. They got rid of the miraculous.

MRS H. You mean . . . got rid of what *you* call the miraculous, but what I would prefer to call natural phenomena, obeying laws they didn't—and we still don't—understand?

P.H. If that is how you prefer to put it. Anyway, just look what they got rid of! In the Church of England liturgy they got rid of the Ministry of Angels. In the Communion Service there isn't one single word about the dead. There are no prayers for the dead, they're all got rid of. There is only one mention of angels in Sursum Corda. In fact, any sort of contact—*living* contact—with the unseen world went right out. And the great majority of the Church of England simply have today no concept at all of an underlying power.

B.N. The power I referred to in my book as the X Force?

P.H. It doesn't really matter what name you give it. I should say it was nearer to what you call 'order'. The point I want to make is that though we claim to be guided by the Holy Spirit, and attend our church committee meetings, the vast majority of us aren't—how shall I say—permeated, illuminated. We just touch our caps to the Holy Spirit in a perfunctory prayer. And nobody ever got anywhere, certainly not to the throne of God, nor to the 'fountain of all wisdom' by touching his cap.

MRS H. May I tell you a silly story? I had a charming mother with a very practical mind. She lived in a village where the parson prided himself on being extremely 'up-to-date', whatever that may mean in spiritual terms. And one day she met him in the street and she couldn't resist the temptation of saying to him: 'Do tell me, Mr Smith, why are you so shocked when I mention the possibility that angels exist? After all, you have a day in the Church which is entirely devoted to St Michael and All Angels.'

P.H. As usual you have hit the nail on the head. And this is what the Fellowship is always saying. You don't believe your own beliefs, so how can you expect others to believe them?

B.N. Can you enlarge on that point a bit? Isn't it rather difficult for people to believe in angels and spirits and miracles in an age of modern science?

P.H. Yes, of course it is. And in my better moments I have a great deal of sympathy with both the reformers and also with those modern scientists who find it hard to believe. After all, we can't have God in the test tube; we can't have spirits monkeying about with scientific experiments. And we don't want a return to witchcraft or the sort of animism which bedevilled so much of primitive life.

B.N. Aren't you beginning to contradict yourself?

P.H. I don't think so. I was only trying to put all this in its historical perspective, because if we forget what happened to the Church in the seventeenth century we can't appreciate what is happening to it in the twentieth. What happened, briefly, was that the Church, by rejecting angelic protection and the intercession of Saints, cut off all contact with the unseen world. And this cutting off created the classic conditions for what I believe is called a 'withdrawal neurosis' such as we find in the early stages of treatment for drug addiction. They had a terrible feeling of psychic insecurity. The great outbreak of witch-hunting in England at this time may well have been due to the withdrawal of a belief in divine protection. People suddenly found that they had to defend *themselves*. And they panicked. And that's the reason for the fear of all those 'ghoulies and ghosties and long leggety beasties and things that go bump in the night', as the Scottish litany has it. Whereas in medieval times there was a sort of psychic balance—the powers of evil were believed to be continually held in check by the angels and ministers of grace who were defending us. Do you mind if I tell a little story, before I hand over to Mrs Heywood?

MRS H. I can always listen to little stories.

P.H. One evening I went into my picture dealer's shop because I'd been attracted by a large oil painting in the window. It was obviously a spiritualist picture. The artist was a Scotch academician called Abercrombie and the title was 'Mother's Voice'. The picture was pretty clearly divided into two halves. The lower half showed a humble interior, a bed by a fireside, a baby boy asleep in the bed, his elder sister leaning over him. She had her face turned upwards, as though she were listening . . . listening very intently.

The upper part of the picture showed her young mother standing over her, with three angels in the background. I don't suggest that this was a supreme masterpiece, but it was painted with reverence and a sort of awe and to me, at any rate, it was beautiful.

The dealer wanted ten pounds for it. I hadn't got ten pounds to spare, so I went away rather sadly without it. A few weeks later I went into the shop again. The picture was still there. The dealer said to me: 'I've had two offers for that picture since you were last here, both from dealers, but I haven't accepted them because they both wanted to cut it in half!' Yes . . . both dealers wanted to keep only the lower half, cutting out the whole vision above, the young mother, the figures of the angels . . . in fact the whole significance and inspiration of the entire design.

B.N. What happened to the picture in the end?

P.H. Well, eventually I traded in another picture I'd bought from him and took it home to my study, where it hangs today. Not a very exciting story I'm afraid, but one might regard it as a parable. It's typical of the modern world. We only want the human interest.

B.N. You mean—we're bored with the supernatural?

MRS H. (in the gentlest of voices). And I wonder if, perhaps, it might not be quite a good thing to be bored with it?

At this point, if this dialogue were being adapted for the theatre, I should probably scribble in a few stage directions, such as 'P.H. and B.N. sit up sharply'. For here there seemed to be a dramatic clash.

'I wonder', she repeated—still in those deceptively gentle tones—'if it might not be quite a good thing to be bored by the supernatural, which is a word that always rather frightens me?'

P.H. I didn't bring in the word. Our host was responsible for that.

B.N. I was only trying to clarify your two points of view.

P.H. Well, that isn't the way to do it. I'm as bored with the supernatural as Rosalind here, if by 'supernatural' you mean a sort of divine Jack-in-the-Box who's always popping up and interfering with the normal law for the benefit of certain individuals.

B.N. I'm not over-fond of the word myself; it just slipped in. But since it *has* slipped in, isn't there a supernatural element in—say—the very fact of making contact with the dead?

MRS H. I don't think I could agree with that. I would have thought it more respectful—yes, *respectful*—to say that if such contact can be made, it must be through obeying laws of nature to which most of us are still blind. Just as 200 years ago we were blind to the laws which make possible a telephone call to New York. I think one reason why so many intellectuals are bored with the supernatural may be that they see the cosmos as an inter-related system, an *ordered* system, a system which makes sense, and the idea of, one might almost say, capricious celestial law-breaking destroys that sense. It would leave me, if I were to accept it, groping about in a sort of vacuum.

P.H. Me too.

B.N. This is getting impossible. Whenever I try to get you at loggerheads you start shaking hands again!

P.H. Because we're not really at loggerheads. Take this argument about law-breaking which arose from your word supernatural.

B.N. I didn't invent it.

P.H. No . . . but it is used a great deal too loosely. I think that what Rosalind and I are really concerned about is getting the scientists to admit that paranormal events take place, even if they can't as yet explain them. If they *do* admit this, then—as Bronowski is reported to have said—they'll have to rethink the whole of their science. Do you agree?

MRS H. I do.

B.N. I was afraid she would! (To Mrs H.) But if we might revert to the question of an after-life, isn't it true that a great many intellectuals feel very differently about it? Isn't it true that some of them have an intuitive certainty that life must go on? Or are you discounting intuition altogether?

MRS H. No, I certainly wouldn't discount intuition in general. Far from it. I'd merely say that it was a specialized form of apprehension which some intellectuals can't bring themselves to accept as evidential unless it is supported by what appear to be the facts. As for the people who can accept survival, I, for one, hope that they may be right. But, may I ask a question which sounds rather heretical?

P.H. Your particular heresies always have a charm of their own.

MRS H. Well then, if it isn't presumptuous, can I ask whether, in the Christian religion, the love of God—which surely should be a virtue or a gift or a grace, whatever you like to call it, *existing in its own right*—may not have become somewhat confused with the desire for personal immortality? And isn't this, even in the most harmless sense of the word, an egotistical desire? What has it to do with true religion—with love for the Divine?

P.H. You really are a remarkable phenomenon. Nail upon nail, bang in the middle. Yes—of course, as far as the highest form of Christian belief is concerned, which involves what we have called the 'love of God', actual evidence of survival isn't of great account. I imagine that any small importance which most mystics might attach to psychic phenomena would be judged solely by the extent to which they could be regarded as rungs on the ladder of spiritual experience. However, I'm not speaking—for the moment at any rate—as a mystic; I'm speaking from the point of view of a practical parson in a parish, trying desperately hard to work for some spiritual improvement in the people among whom I minister, and I'm totally convinced that *unless* we can tell them—and tell them from knowledge and conviction—that there *is* a continuity of this life after death . . . *unless* we can assure them that they will go on into the many mansions of our Father, we're simply wasting our time.

MRS H. Yes, I see your point and I respect it, if that doesn't sound too presumptuous.

B.N. But how many parsons feel as you do?

P.H. It would be easier to say how many didn't! Look at the Bishop of Woolwich. John Robinson, if I understand him rightly, won't have anything to do with psychic phenomena as evidence for survival. He doesn't seem interested. He doesn't seem to realize that these minor phenomena—if we choose to regard them as such—might play a tremendous part in forcing men to face up to all the *major* phenomena which are enshrined in the Christian religion. Let me put it like this. If you can prove that *one* voice has spoken from beyond the grave, that *one* spirit has manifested itself, mustn't this compel any man of the smallest intelligence to ask himself if there may not be other voices, many voices, countless millions of voices? He *must* ask himself this question, and no man who has asked it will ever be quite the same again. But John Robinson won't see this. He merely says: 'What *we* are interested in is eternal life.' To which I reply: 'All right. And what, pray, are the criteria for eternal life? Have *you* got it? I'd really like to know. Have bishops got eternal life? And what about archdeacons? Have they got it, or is it just the newly-ordained curates?'

B.N. I think you should have another glass of wine.

P.H. Thank you. And I sometimes think that the Church of England should have a glass of wine, several glasses indeed, just to put the fire back into its veins. Isn't that why the churches aren't full? They haven't any divine intoxication, and the average man can't get intoxicated out of books. In fact the churches of England—and I believe that this goes for Protestant churches all over the world, including America—are today doing precisely what the Jewish authorities were doing at the time of Our Lord. They have become People of the Book.

MRS H. You mean, they speak as scribes and not from personal experience?

P.H. Exactly. What we want is a sort of Christian existentialism, where people speak from personal experience.

MRS H. All the same, isn't there sometimes a tendency among enthusiastic spiritualists to attribute to intervention from the other world phenomena which could much more simply be attributed to telepathy between living people? And that perhaps it isn't quite fair to blame the Church for mistrusting this tendency?

P.H. I couldn't agree with you more. But I'm not really trying to 'sell' spiritualism to the Church. What I'm trying to do—what all of us in the Churches' Fellowship are trying to do—is to interest them in psychic phenomena *generally*. Because if they could realize that these phenomena were occurring *today,* they would automatically relate them to the phenomena of two thousand years ago. And I think that this would serve two purposes. It would make the 'miracles' of the past more vivid and more actual, and it would make the phenomena of the present more . . . well, more miraculous.

B.N. You said that you aren't trying to 'sell' spiritualism to the Church. But you *are* trying to 'sell' psychical research. What is the difference?

P.H. All the difference in the world. Spiritualism, even though it mayn't have any theology or written doctrine in the form of a creed, *is* a form of religion, or at least has the makings of one. Psychical research is nothing of the sort. It's a pioneer movement of inquiry into territories where the Church is vitally concerned and we should be passionately interested in what the pioneers discover. Because whatever they discover I'm quite convinced that it will reinforce the beliefs we already hold. But if you want a justification of psychical research, *per se,* you must apply to Mrs Heywood.

MRS H. Before answering that, may I make one comment? Canon Pearce-Higgins is naturally interested in the kind of psychic perception which appears to bear directly on survival after death. I think we should be careful not to forget that the existence of mundane psychic perception, of telepathy between the living for instance, for which, to my mind, there is coercive evidence, does not *necessarily* imply survival. It need not differ in kind from sensory perception, in the sense, I mean, that they're both, in their different ways, tools enabling us to react to our environment. Also, I can't see what such a tool has to do with what I should like to call 'spiritual quality'. The use you make of it, perhaps, but not the tool itself. I gather that you agree?

P.H. Very much so. In fact one can imagine such a tool being used to manipulate our fellow-men to our own advantage.

MRS H. As far as 'justifications' for psychical research are obvious; that any extension of knowledge about ourselves and our environment must be of value. It must broaden our minds, don't you think? Take the discovery that our brains are very delicate electrical instruments. Doesn't that make us see ourselves from a new angle, as being literally part of what appears to be a vast electrical system, the universe itself?

B.N. We seem to be getting back to Mesmer.

MRS H. I don't know enough about Mesmer to comment. But take the change of outlook from the days when scientists thought they knew that the basic particles of matter were solid little billiard-ball atoms. I read somewhere not long ago that now we must think of those particles as no more than 'the concentration of a certain amount of electrical charge into a mathematical point'. I also read in a recent scientific review that nowadays 'every particle has to be thought of as having an influence throughout the *whole* of space. And space itself has become very different from the infinite ocean in which matter used to sail about like ships.' What's more, a physicist told me the other day that certain particles appear able, for a fractional moment, to go back in time.

B.N. Go back in time? I should have thought that was a classic example of breaking the rules . . . and, if it is . . . that it might invalidate your objection to miracles.

MRS H. (laughing). I don't see why. Surely all it means is that *we* don't yet know all the rules. But perhaps we needn't worry. Another physicist has since told me that this was only a convenient way of *talking* about the particles.

B.N. I'm totally out of my depth.

MRS H. So am I.

B.N. So may we have your second justification for psychical research?

MRS H. I mentioned the change in the outlook of physicists, because it may help us to envisage the possibility that at some subconscious level all men are interlinked and constantly interacting with one another. It may hint that we are not the encapsulated little entities that our surface minds—particularly those of Western man—would like to think. If that is so, it ought surely to affect our conduct as individuals—from the most egotistic angle, it could mean that the love or hate we send out mentally may bounce back, reinforced, upon ourselves—and also, incidentally, it ought to inspire our efforts when we cease to act as individuals and join together in international organizations such as the U.N. I mean, if we are literally members of one another, the sooner we know it the better, don't you think? Even from the most egocentric point of view, it might at least discourage us from dropping bombs on each other.

P.H. That word 'encapsulated' is astonishingly apt. And what you said about *not* being encapsulated was presumably what Jesus meant when He said: 'I am the vine and ye are the branches.' I'm delighted you brought up this point for I've felt for a long time that much of modern psychology tends to encapsulate us. Look at Freud . . . even when he was delving down into the depths of the subconscious mind he never got away from *my* subconscious mind, *your* subconscious mind, and we were still, as it were, analysing processes which were supposed to go on inside the cranium. Whereas E.S.P. and dream experiences and so on would seem to indicate, as the poet Vaughan says, that 'Some dreams transcend their wonted themes and into glory peep'.

MRS H. Yes, Freud may have kept within the individual. But Jung didn't.

P.H. I was brought up on heavy doses of Freud, which I found quite terrifying and depressing, and only later was introduced to Jung, whom I still don't fully understand. But he has a far wider concept of the basic roots of personality as being interlinked in a common unconscious. I think that McTaggart was on the right lines when he posited an infinite multitude of spirits—of units of consciousness. Matter does not exist apart from human consciousness. I've just been reading a review of a ridiculous book by Dr Nkrumah, a most alarming book in which he put in very crude terms what he thinks is the Marxist case. He says that matter is the ultimate thing in the Universe. Now this is just something that we cannot accept.

MRS H. You said *human* consciousness.

P.H. Ah yes . . . what a horrible critic you are! Of course —please God—I hope that there are other units of consciousness in this Universe which are infinitely more developed than human consciousness. You are quite right and I'm absolutely with you. Angels, and archangels and all the company of Heaven . . .

At that point something went wrong with the tape, and it degenerates into a jumble of distorted words and phrases. If I were presenting this dialogue as a polished party piece I should have endeavoured to tidy it up, and to contrive some sort of dramatic 'curtain'. But it seems better to leave it as it stands, ending in the air. For that, I suppose, is how all earthly arguments must end, drifting up to the skies like the smoke from the dying fire.

To this fire I returned when they had gone, and gave the logs a kick. The smoke changed from grey to silver, specked with sparks of gold. So it had been tonight. One gave the words a twist, the colour of the conversation changed, and now and then there was a spark of wisdom.

But where did it all go . . . the conversation, and the cloudy wisps of smoke from the apple logs? Where indeed? For the smoke, perhaps, one might answer. Nothing in Nature is lost, they tell us, nothing really dies. So when the smoke drifted through the chimney, from its dark, man-made funnel, and became part of the cold, infinite airs around it—when it joined the night, adding its little tithe of fragrance to the multitudinous scents of the world, it still went on—in what tenuous shapes of form one did not know. One would never know, and it was past midnight, and it was too late to go on puzzling. But somehow, I felt that the smoke from the apple logs had mingled with the argument, and had something to say about it . . . something that was neither inapposite nor melancholy.

For they were telling a story of beauty that had died but still lingered on, of a far-off spring that had vanished, but was eternally renewed, of an essence, a vitality, a spirit, that was charted to the stars.

Postscript. Although I have resisted the temptation to give an artificial 'curtain' to this conversation it seemed unsatisfactory—and unfair to the participators—to deny them the privilege of a final word. This they have kindly provided, in the form of two letters which throw a vivid flash of light on their personalities, before they step off the stage.

Rosalind Heywood. My final word is that on such a topic no word of mine could possibly be final. I feel as if I were groping along a tunnel, towards a flickering glimmer of very distant light. No, I think I ought to have said that the light may well be all round us, but that our eyes, like those of newborn kittens, can't take it. So we keep them shut.

I wonder what is the real difference between Canon Pearce-Higgins and me? It isn't that I share the current determinist materialist outlook: old-fashioned matter is all in all; psi phenomena can't occur; so that's that. I don't. I'm intuitively convinced that something I vaguely call spiritual quality permeates an ordered universe, and I hope that we humans will gradually become more aware of it.

But this kind of discussion is out of my class. Let's drop to the human level. Here, for the sake of your dialogue, I wish that there could be a real clash between Canon Pearce-Higgins and me. As a dramatist you must have been longing for some sort of *scène à faire,* and I suspect that you tried to build one around that word 'supernatural'! But he likes the idea of the Deity as a sort of 'divine Jack-in-the-Box', as he put it, as little as I do—and whatever our differences, I believe he shares my feeling that the world is more astounding than any miracle. I want us all to strive for grace to see the spirit shining through it—to learn to *look* at a beetle, a baby, a crystal, a leaf, a mountain, a star—or even at a molecule under an electron microscope—and then, simply because we can't help it, break into our own version of the *Benedicite* in response to the glory of what we see. Not long ago I heard a saintly Christian talk of 'this ordinary world'. I wanted to scream. I think I did. But, you know, what I've been saying sounds to me very like intellectual arrogance. I'm probably just playing with words. Different types of eye may need different tools to jerk them open, and in some cases seeming miracles may well be the right ones. Who am I to lay down what tools other people should use? I've more than enough to do hunting for one which could prise open my own stubbornly closed eyes.

Canon Pearce-Higgins. As to a final word: I have always considered Rosalind to be a remarkable phenomenon. I wrote in a review of her first book that the evidence she adduces would convince anyone but the author of the reality of survival! But I believe that there is a fundamental unity underlying both her and my approach. She is concerned with value, perhaps as experienced existentially. She has a fine sense of 'quality' of life and thought, and this she prizes above everything. She does this intuitively and without any metaphysical background. But this sense of quality of living is more or less what Christianity means by 'eternal life'—it is the quality of life which makes survival worth having. Bare survival might be awful indeed, without that quality. I suspect that the only difference between us is that I enclose a similar set of values within the metaphysical framework of a somewhat liberalized Christianity. (Which I think some of my colleagues would hardly deem to be Christian at all.)

I would like to say one last thing about survival—our belief or disbelief in it—as it affects not only the Church but the whole of the modern world. Would you not agree that the wide-spread decline in any sort of belief in an after-life may be largely responsible for many of the major horrors of our present century? I don't need to be reminded of the brutalities that have been committed in the past, in the name of religion . . . but does history record any brutalities quite so gross as those which were committed at Belsen? And have there ever been any tyrannies so ruthless, carried through with such scientific precision, as we have seen during the rise and practice of communism? I can't believe that these appalling things could have been done by men who had even a shadow of a belief in an after-life . . . if they had even a momentary suspicion that there might be some sort of heaven or some sort of hell. If you tell me that I am merely saying that 'if there hadn't been a heaven or a hell it would be necessary to invent one', simply as a carrot for the good little boys and a bogey for the bad ones, I suppose I must accept the criticism, but it really isn't as simple as that. It is that without a future life, there is really no 'accountability'—no responsibility for human beings, and no hope, as Kingsley put it at the end of that wonderful essay on the hereafter, *The Water Babies,* which every adult ought to read, that 'somehow, somewhere, somewhen things will be put right'.

17. IN MY END IS MY BEGINNING

This is a book to which there can be no end; as each new avenue opens we discover that it stretches to infinity; and in our present state of knowledge the avenues are narrow and dimly lit. We may make a little groping progress but all round is the dark uncharted forest, teeming with mysteries, echoing with strange voices speaking a language to which no human dictionary holds the key.

Is it worth while trying to explore these avenues at all? To me it seems so. Even a tiny clearing in the forest, catching the transient light of a distant star, may serve to guide the footsteps of those who follow after. Whether we have made any 'clearings' in the preceding pages must remain a matter of opinion. I think that we may have made a few, though I should be the last to quarrel with any critic who complains that they do not link up into any single avenue, and that they represented only a random hacking away at the undergrowth, rather than an expedition scientifically conducted with maps and compasses. But there *are* no maps nor compasses. The explorer in these territories has to make his own charts and set his course by the star of his own personality.

The word 'personality' suggests that there may perhaps be a connecting link after all, a thread that binds our pages together, however loosely. For always, in our examination of what we called the X Force, we found ourselves obliged to study it through the medium of a specific *personality*. The energy that Mesmer saw as a universal 'fluid' encompassing the earth and its inhabitants had been recognized by many others throughout the centuries, but it needed Mesmer, like a sort of human lightning conductor, to attract it, to make it flow through his own fingers for the benefit of mankind. So it is with a man like Michael Ash. The energy which radiates from him—an energy of which I am only one of many personal beneficiaries—is flowing down Harley Street, and indeed through every street of the world, but it seems to flow only through a very few doors, into a very few consulting rooms. Ash, quite simply, calls it the power of God, but even he, in a moment of humour, when he was discussing some of the other workers in these fields, observed: 'We are all prima donnas.'

Prima donnas, prophets, seers, star-gazers—is it of much consequence how we call them? What matters, surely, is that we should recognize their existence, and try to learn from them. They may be more numerous than we suspect. Obviously, healers of the quality of Harry Edwards do not grow on every tree, but Edwards is by no means the only healer practising in modern Britain. At a conservative estimate there are several thousands. Doubtless, a number of these are bogus, but we must expect such persons and it is foolish to be too greatly offended by them. Even in the dusty crowds that followed in the footsteps of Christ there must have been many charlatans, trying to catch a flicker of His radiance, palm it off in their own fingers, and sell it for gold. For all I know, there may have been so much gold lingering about, carelessly spilt from His lightest utterance and His smallest gesture, that they may sometimes, in their scavenging, have served a useful purpose.

I do not believe that the persons I have introduced into this book, as recipients and transmitters of the X Force, have been charlatans. Nor do I believe—and this is the vital point —that they are necessarily so far removed from the common run of humanity. We are all recipients of the X Force, but we might also be in our varying degrees, transmitters. True, a woman like Evelyn Penrose, with her miraculous gifts, only comes once in a life-time; if we can think of the psychic world in terms of the theatre, the ballet, or the opera she is a Duse, a Pavlova, or a Patti. But Miss Penrose does not think of herself as a being set apart; indeed, as we have seen, she is so acutely conscious of the forces that have used her and flowed through her, all her life, that she is impatient for others to use them, and even instructs us in some simple rules which will help us to do so.

Yet again, although a man like de la Warr, with his daz-

zling cadenzas of theory and his psycho-scientific arias which
are sometimes pitched in a key too high for most of us to
follow . . . though he may have prima donna qualities he
has none of a prima donna's exclusiveness. His whole life
has been devoted to proving the *universality* of the X Force
and to devising techniques by which all of us can put ourselves in harmony with it. Perhaps the prima donna metaphor is most apposite in the sphere of telepathy. Here, the
experiments of Rhine and of the Society for Psychical Research have proved conclusively—as conclusively as most
reasonable men would demand—the existence of a limited
number of men and women with exceptional gifts of 'paranormal cognition'. But though these may be the spot-lit stars
in this most exciting of all Theatres of Experiment, an
equally impressive body of reasearch is available to prove
that a very large percentage of the members of the audience
have also had some telepathic experience. And since the audience comprises all the members of the human family it
seems sad that so few 'talent-spotters' are moving among
them. For every telepathic experience, in its way, is a glimpse
into a world of which we know all too little.

Now that we have introduced the metaphor of the prima
donna I should like to indulge in a moment's purely personal
fantasy. I have always had an instinct that the key to these
mysteries, if it is ever found—the skeleton key that will un-
lock all the doors, enabling us to wander through all the
rooms of the many mansions, drawing up the blinds and let-
ting in the light—will be discovered in the realm of music.
Man draws nearest to God with a song. He may build temples that stretch to the clouds, and catch on his canvas a light
that never shone on land or sea, but only with a song can he
soar to the stars. We must remember, too, that in the temples
that he builds and the pictures that he paints there is a
restricting element, a *spatial* element. The Parthenon may
still stand proudly on the moonlit Acropolis but its shadow
falls only within the area of its building; and even the most
beautiful pictures, though their image may linger in our
minds, are imprisoned in their galleries, caged within their
golden frames. But music is everywhere, drifting through
every nook and cranny of the world. Even if we cannot hear
it because we may be momentarily deprived of the instruments that bring it into our ken, modern science has proved
that it is in fact in the air around us, all the time. The mountains are echoing to the fugues of Bach, on and through all

eternity; and in every country lane the wild roses are dancing to the melodies of Mozart.

This, of course, is pure fantasy, and to many it will sound sheer nonsense. But to me, and perhaps a few others, it may make some sort of sense even though it takes a thousand centuries to prove it. If all art 'tends to the condition of music' so does all passion and all prayer. And when the passion has died and the words of the prayer are forgotten, the *music* of the prayer may linger on.

A last word. As a practical person, an elector and a taxpayer, I should like to make a concrete suggestion: that we should create here and now a Ministry for Psychical Research sustained by public funds, of which the present Society of the same name would form the nucleus. And that attached to this Ministry there should be subsidiary departments, on however modest a scale, for research into every branch of the kindred phenomena which we have been examining—spiritual healing, radionics, divining for water, oil and metals, and, of course, telepathy.

Before such a suggestion is dismissed as ridiculous, as a squandering of public money on matters of small importance, perhaps the critic would answer one or two simple questions. What subject is more important than death? The cheap and obvious answer, of course, is 'life'. Indeed, this monosyllabic retort was once made to me, with some contempt, by one of the most prosperous and publicized of our younger dramatists. I suggested that he was forgetting the tricks of his trade. Life is a drama and no drama can be written or enacted without a constant reference to the final curtain. The first line of Act One, even if it is only the cry of a baby in the wings, is—theatrically—a desolate and meaningless whimper if it does not in some way or other connect with the final line of Act Three, even if it is only a grunt from a nonagenarian as he is wheeled off in his invalid chair. This does not mean that during our lives we should be constantly preoccupied with thoughts of death, but it must surely mean that the sensible man or woman must be concerned with what happens after the fall of the curtain, and must welcome every intelligent effort to find out. Those who are able to accept in toto the tenets of the great religions, untroubled by even a momentary doubt of their literal validity, will have no need of this extra reassurance, but there are others, and they are probably in the majority, who would welcome it.

Can we gain this reassurance? We could at least try. But we are not trying. As far as I am aware, not a penny of the taxpayer's money is being expended on any form of psychical research—the only sort of research which may hold the answer to the most important questions we can ask ourselves during our passage through this world. Is not this a ludicrous, indeed a tragic, situation? We are spending astronomical sums on a race to the moon in order—once we have reached it—to be in a more favourable position to blow up the earth. Possibly, before doing so, our scientists may be able to send back some reports of a minor interest concerning the nature of the lunar atmosphere and the composition of the volcanic soil of those ghostly landscapes. Would it not be infinitely more rewarding for the human race if some small fraction of these sums was devoted to an exploration of the psychic atmosphere of our own earth and the secrets of our own soil, and of man's mystic relation to it?

Which brings me back to my young dramatist, with his facile suggestion that life is 'more important than death'. Even if this observation has any truth, even if we accept the melancholy thesis that the whole story of life is told in a single sentence, scribbled on a blank sheet of paper, and bounded by an uncompromising full stop, we might at least try to make the best of it while we are here. How can we possibly do so when the whole apparatus of government— ours and every other country's—is constructed on the assumption that such phenomena as we have been discussing in these pages have no existence? One of these phenomena— spirit-healing—is particularly worthy of consideration in our own Welfare State, which is rapidly developing into a sort of gigantic cash chemist where nobody pays any cash except the taxpayer. If it is even vaguely possible that in spirit-healing we have a powerful channel of natural therapy, why has it never been suggested that even a halfpenny of public money should go towards exploring this possibility? The British swallow enough aspirins to sink a ship and rub in enough ointments to smear the face of the earth, but they still seem to have a permanent headache, and if they are not at the moment afflicted with rheumatism they confidently look forward with a sort of masochistic anticipation to the day when they will be enjoying it.

And yet, there is overwhelming evidence, of which this

book has given only the briefest indication, that the spirit-healers *do* cure headaches and rheumatism—to put their achievements at the lowest. Or that literally hundreds of thousands of afflicted persons are under the firm impression that they have been cured by spiritual means, which seems to me much the same thing. This evidence is available. Why is nothing done about it?

Again, why has there never been any official recognition of the faculty of water-divining, and of 'dowsing' in general, for oils and minerals? In the undeveloped areas of the Commonwealth incalculable riches are hidden, and vast sums are annually expended in an effort to locate these riches, using the orthodox methods of geological engineering. If the same results might be obtained, more quickly and at a fraction of the cost, by means of dowsing, why is no effort made to do so? Must we put the blame on those familiar villains of all industrial society—'vested interests'? Or is it simply a question of sheer human stupidity?

All these questions really resolve themselves into a single question: 'Will you come over to the side of Mr Sludge? Will you admit that there may be something in it, tricks and all?' In the present climate of public opinion the answer would almost certainly be an emphatic 'No'. Any Minister of Agriculture who was rash enough to be photographed holding a hazel twig would make himself a public laughing stock, and any Minister of Transport who dared to investigate Professor Maby's theories regarding the connection between road accidents and hidden streams would be hounded out of public life. Any Minister of Health who was even vaguely suspected of corresponding with a spirit-healer would lose the votes of ten million dedicated aspirin-swallowers. As for any Minister, in any department whatsoever, who gave public recognition to the work of de la Warr, or even ventured to peep inside the Box . . . the furies let loose by Pandora would be as nothing to those which would assail him.

And there I will draw a line, having amply fulfilled the promise given to the reader in an earlier chapter—to write this book badly. All the same, I still think it was worth writing, even if its sole result is to tempt some other author, more learned and more competent, to slash it to pieces. That kindred books will be written in increasing numbers seems reasonably certain, for every advance of science makes us re-draw the maps of our minds, and re-adjust the sights of our

telescopes as we peer into more and more distant horizons.
And as each author comes to his final chapter, he may find
himself echoing, as I do, the words of Rossetti:

> . . . from this wave-washed mound
> Into the furthest flood-brim look with me;
> Then reach on with thy thought till it be drown'd:
> Miles and miles distant though the last line be,
> Still, leagues beyond those leagues, there is more sea.

APPENDIX

The de la Warr Box. The Box which we are about to open is not the 'Multi-Oscillator Unit and Detector' mentioned in Chapter Eight but the comparatively simple diagnostic instrument which, as we have seen, is in wide use throughout modern Britain.

In opening it I feel like a sort of anti-climactic Pandora, dismayed by the fact that when the lid came off nothing particularly unpleasant emerged. It came off for me on the afternoon of April 16th, 1964, in the Delawarr Laboratories, and this was all I saw.

Firstly:

Nine variable rheostats calibrated from 1 to 10 connected in series with a detector unit consisting of a thin sheet of rubber over a metal plate.

This description is from the pen of Dr Tertius Watson, author of an admirable pamphlet on radiesthesia.

Let us put this into comparatively plain English. For 'rheostats' read 'resonators'. They are in fact thin wires arranged in a fan-shaped formation. Do not think in terms of electricity. Think of 'rapport'. Think, indeed, almost in terms of music, as if those delicately adjusted wires were made to catch the echo of harmony or discord, of health or disease.

Return to Dr Watson. 'These rheostats are not electrically powered. The patient may be directly linked to the instrument or a blood-spot may be used. In the latter case the patient may be *any distance away*.'

I have italicized the words 'any distance away' to emphasize the fact that we are already outside the time dimension and that we must eliminate from our minds any questions of 'vibrations' or 'waves'. Supposing that the blood-spot in the machine belongs to a man who at the moment of diagnosis is in South Africa, the 'rapport' between the blood-spot and the man is instantaneous. This point is important because the very fact that the Box has any mechanical gadgets at all suggests that there must be some form of 'radio' connection. This erroneous impression is enhanced by what comes next—the rubber pad.

We have already referred to this device in the body of the text, so that in the present section we need merely remind the reader that when the operator is stroking this pad the rubber suddenly becomes sticky to his fingers. This does not imply any change in the consistency of the rubber itself; it does not become moist or taut or anything like that. What happens is that *the thought of the operator changes the signals on the skin.*

And there, after a deep sigh and painful swallow, we might leave the matter, filing it away in our minds under M for Mysteries. However, I believe that we may, at least partially, unveil the mystery, by considering it from a quite different angle.

If, as I have already suggested, many of life's problems can be understood in terms of music, and if we try to give to these mysteries a musical interpretation we may not think it too far-fetched to regard the de la Warr operators, so to speak, as violinists, playing on instruments for which the world is not yet ready, in harmonies of a complexity which have never been previously attempted. This interpretation I believe to be not so far from the truth, especially when one remembers that these imaginary violinists are making a music that cannot be heard, in the same way that the Boxes appear to be affecting physical tissues in a manner which cannot be seen. (Except, of course, in their results.)

However, the fact that we cannot *hear* the music nor *see* the therapy—in the sense, that is to say, that we can see notes of a composition or the scars of an operation—does not invalidate the analogy. The room in which we sit at this moment is uproarious with music from all over the world; the thing we call the 'ether' is in a perpetual, ear-splitting din of conflicting symphonies and serried ranks of shrieking sopranos; all we have to do to prove this alarming fact is to buy a hundred radio sets and turn them all on at once. The radio sets, in themselves, are incapable of creating the softest whisper, they merely enable us to hear what is there already. So it is, I believe, *mutatis mutandis,* with the Boxes. The main difference between the radio set and the Box is that whereas anybody can 'get', say, Radio Luxembourg by turning a knob, it takes a skilled operator, holding a particular thought with great concentration, to 'get' a patient on the other side of the world.

The Book of Rates. Here we come to an even more difficult matter—so difficult, indeed, that even de la Warr's personal 'simplified' explanation of it will baffle the average reader. The Book of Rates is not, of course, an integral part of the Box, it is merely used in conjunction with it. If you open one of these books at the laboratories you will find that it is divided into sections dealing with every known part of the human body, and every known disease to which the flesh is heir, from a simple pain in the big toe to the most esoteric form of tropical food poisoning. Against each of these conditions is set a number. You will also find an equally comprehensive catalogue of mental conditions, from a 'standard' inferiority complex—if there is such a thing—to the most convoluted case of schizophrenia.

Thus:

Inflammation of the Lower Intestines   6435
Acute Persecution Complex   2340

There are no less than seven thousand of these numbers.

When we remember that the combination of each and every one of them has been arrived at by the de la Warrs through many long years of monotonous experiment—for most of us would find it extremely monotonous to sit in front of a box, year after year, stroking a rubber membrane and fiddling about with a lot of dials—you are forced to one of two conclusions. Either the de la Warrs and their staff are exceptionally perverted lunatics, with a strong streak of masochism, or they have been constantly sustained and inspired by the conviction that they are working in fields of great importance. In investigating matters such as these it seems the height of folly to ignore the human element—the personality and background of the chief protagonists.

But what *are* these 'numbers'? Here we will let de la Warr speak for himself.

Our 7,000 dial settings, or rates, are pattens of frequencies that enable the Instrument to be pre-set to the requisite energy pattern for the thought that is about to be used.

This we can follow . . . just. But when he develops the theme the average reader may feel that he is—in his own words—'unreadable'. However, after all my own fumbling and groping, it is only fair that he should be given the floor for a moment.

He continues:

> These frequencies contain many harmonics and sub-harmonics and the actual frequencies cannot be measured. This is Radionics and enables criticism to be levelled at us. So in Paraphysics electronic oscillators are used to enable *precise* frequencies to be used. This is frankly more cumbersome and expensive but it is more scientific and has enabled good progress to be made with the research. Paraphysics uses 'frequency runs' of many figures whereas the 'rates' in Radionics are much shorter sequences. We are currently adding to both methods.

We will not attempt to comment upon this. But in the next paragraph we come—comparatively—down to earth. Like many other beginners I was still obsessed by the idea of *distance,* and indeed a little in awe of it. To put it crudely, it seemed more remarkable that an operator should be able to contact a man who was in South Africa than a man who was in the next room . . . just as it seems more remarkable to be able to telephone from London to San Francisco than from London to Brighton.

Here is de la Warr's corrective to this misconception:

> The very idea of range or distance is quite meaningless in the paraphysical realm in which we are endeavouring to gain understanding. Can a thought form have actual physical dimension? What, for example, is a 'large' thought? If rapport is instantaneous than there is no travelling of *movement* or *energy* between the points of rapport.

That is clear enough, at any rate in theory, however difficult it may sometimes seem in application. It is merely another reminder of the fact that though we may be sitting in a laboratory we are outside the realms of time and space.